Maximise
Confic

How To Lose Your Phone Fear and Win More Customers.

Includes Straightforward Approach™ The powerful telemarketing system guaranteed to get results!

Robbie Stepney FInstSMM

1st Edition
Maximise Your Phone Confidence™ Publishing
The Colchester Centre, Hawkins Road, Colchester,
Essex CO2 8JX United Kingdom

Maximise Your Phone Confidence™

How To Lose Your Phone Fear and Win More Customers.

Includes Straightforward Approach™ the powerful telemarketing system guaranteed to get results!

Robbie Stepney FInstSMM

First published in Great Britain by Maximise Your Phone Confidence™ Publishing 2015

Dedication

This book is dedicated to my very special family

My beautiful wife Nicky, son Jay, and daughter Amy-May

Thanks for your love and support, I'm very lucky (and you don't know how lucky you are!) Robbie x

Special Thanks

Special Thanks also to Mark Rhodes for writing the foreword to this book. You can learn more about Mark's work as an international author, speaker, coach and mentor at www.MarkRhodes.com

Contents

Part Three: Securing sales appointments and dealing with objections...........................143

About the author

Robbie Stepney was born in Romford Essex, and is a passionate ambassador for his county. He is on a mission to help people in business to develop high levels of confidence in using the telephone to win more business.

Attendees at his training sessions are given practical strategies to help them make calls with confidence to people they do not know (yet) as well as maximising the potential of the phone when calling warmer contacts through effective follow up.

He also personifies what many people mean when they talk about someone being a "natural salesperson" and has spent over 20 years using the phone as the first point of contact to initiate, develop and progress new business relationships. He has in that time been trained by some of the very best household names in the world of B2B sales and continues his own professional development by regularly attending industry conferences and events worldwide to keep informed on the very latest trends in telephone sales lead generation.

Robbie has spent his career in the trenches at the very sharp end of new business development. His first telephone sales job was at the age of 16 when on his own he took the paid for advertising section of an industrial equipment magazine from 16 pages to over 100 in less than 2 years! He has also known what it's like to be selling on commission only over the phone calling Senior Executives to sell media opportunities where success was the only outcome that was going to pay his mortgage.

Working in a wide range of direct sales positions across different industry sectors including advertising, media and automotive, he's made literally thousands and thousands of calls resulting in either a face to face sales appointment for him or others. Along the way he's additionally uncovered thousands more qualified sales leads.

Robbie is passionate about the power of the telephone, in particular in giving people the confidence they need to start making more calls, more effectively. As well as being MD of award winning B2B telemarketing Company Calls That Count Limited that he founded in 2008 Robbie is a speaker on the topic of winning business over the phone. His engaging presentations are packed with real life practical tools and tips developed from hours and hours of "working the phones".

Having distilled the very best of what he's learned through hands on experience throughout his career he's developed his unique **Maximise Your Phone Confidence**™ system upon which this book is based.

Under his **Maximise Your Phone Confidence**™ brand Robbie delivers bespoke on site company training, open workshops and coaching programmes helping individuals, business owners and Company sales teams to maximise their effectiveness on the telephone. At the heart of what he teaches is **Straightforward Approach**™ his own unique and powerful telemarketing system which he guarantees will get results for those people who have the courage to push their comfort zones and increase their activity levels. **Straightforward Approach**™ is the distillation of his years of telephone marketing and sales experience outlined in a format that makes it easy whatever your previous experience or skill level, to start making calls and start making things happen.

He has a particular interest in helping owners of small businesses who find the activity of calling people they don't know (or even those they do!) daunting to say the least. They may never have had to be a salesperson before and it's an uncomfortable place for them. They are able to tap into Robbie's knowledge and start winning new business quickly after attending one of his training or coaching sessions.

However, he's equally at home talking to a team of seasoned sales professionals who want a fresh perspective on how to get the most from their telephone calls, or people in job roles other than sales where speaking to clients or potential clients on the phone is an important part of each day.

His philosophy when explaining the secret to making effective phone calls is very disarming in its simplicity. "There are as many opinions on how to sell over the phone as there are numbers in the telephone directory. However, all the techniques in the world don't matter and won't help you if you don't have the confidence to pick the phone up in the first place. That's where you should start. **Maximise Your Phone Confidence**™ first, and the rest will just happen naturally. In order to do that you need a system that is easy and straightforward to follow and that's exactly what you get with **Straightforward Approach**™"

Away from work Robbie is a family man married to Nicky, and Dad to son Jay and daughter Amy-May. He loves all sport particularly cycling, ice hockey, boxing and football.

Official Disclaimer

This book is designed to provide information about the subject matter covered. The reader accepts and understands that the publisher and author provide the information on the understanding that they are doing so purely to supplement the considerable amount of other information available on the subject to the reader, and further that the reader will seek all necessary professional advice to ensure that both the content and strategies outlined are suitable for implementation within their specific business.

This book is not presented nor is it intended to be perceived as being a definitive manual on the subject.

The publisher and author encourage the reader to seek out other sources of information on the subject to gain a thorough and broad understanding of the topic.

Telemarketing is most definitely not a magic wand to transform someone's business overnight. Anyone implementing telemarketing into their business as part of an overall marketing strategy must be prepared to work hard at it, to hone their approach and skill set over time, and accept that anything worthwhile doing takes energy, enthusiasm, and gritty determination.

Every effort has been made to ensure accuracy of spelling and grammar but we apologise upfront for any typographical errors that you may find.

Finally, we want the reader of this book to be both entertained and educated. The author and **Maximise Your Phone Confidence**™ Publishing shall have neither liability nor responsibility to any person or entity with respect to any loss or damage caused or allegedly to be caused directly or indirectly by the information contained in this book.

If for any reason, the reader is not happy to be bound by the above then no hard feelings, just return the book to the publisher for a full no quibble no question refund.

Robbie's Disclaimer

I've written this book to help you to become more confident and successful on the phone and to help your sales revenues to grow in a big way.

Read the book, use what you like, and leave anything you don't. The main thing is to have an open mind and give this your very best shot.

One other "wealth warning"

Not picking up your telephone to talk with people to promote your business can seriously damage your wealth.

OK great now let's start winning some business...

Foreword By Mark Rhodes

They say one of the biggest fears people experience in life is that of public speaking. I should know I once had such a fear of public speaking I smashed up my own car to avoid a 2 minute talk to 12 people. These days I speak for an hour or more with 1,000 people in the room and love every minute of it. Yes a massive change has happened in me due to developing my mindset and skill set in the area of public speaking.

Right up there on the list of fears most business people have (although less spoken about) is the fear of using the phone, especially in the situation of selling or looking to win more business. In fact people tend to have this fear of the phone in most situations where they want something from the person they are calling.

The thing is though the fear of the phone and making calls has far more impact on someone's life and success than the fear of public speaking. Why? Because most people only need to speak in public occasionally but they often need to make calls daily! What's more, making or not making these calls directly relates to the amount of income they generate or level of success they have.

These days people feel they can get away without using the phone and use email, online advertising, websites and social media. However for most people this isn't the solution. All of these methods give little feedback on why the prospect isn't taking action and you have no opportunity to turn the situation around.

In a phone call you get live feedback and opinion, you can hear the hesitation in the persons voice and add more information to make them feel more comfortable. If they don't respond as you'd like, you have the chance to find out why and possibly even change their mind.

So, just like I transformed my fear of public speaking you can transform your fear of using the phone. Just do what I did - develop your mindset and skill set around using the phone.

How? By reading and applying what you learn in this book.

Robbie has taken his years of experience in the arena of using the phone to win business and gives you all of the skill set and mindset information you need to get on the phone with confidence and start getting better results from the calls you make.

Mark Rhodes
Author of "Think Your Way To Success" and "How To Talk To Absolutely Anyone"
www.markrhodes.com

Introduction from the author

Why becoming more confident on the phone will be great for your business

First of all, welcome, and congratulations on being willing to spend some time getting to grips with an activity that could literally transform you sales revenues, sales pipeline, and ultimately your business. This book is based on my very own powerful and unique **Maximise Your Phone Confidence**™ system incorporating **Straightforward Approach**™ and acts as a guide to making really effective sales and marketing calls for people with little or no prior experience, or even those who are experienced but looking for fresh ideas. It has been written for everyone that has a genuine interest in becoming more confident on a telephone enabling them to hit their targets and reach their objectives. In particular I have a real passion for helping the business owners amongst you who to be frank find the prospect of picking up a telephone to make a "sales" call something that brings you out in a cold sweat. You feel uneasy about it, about "cold calling" someone, about having to be "the salesperson". You may even feel uneasy when using the phone to make a follow up call to someone you met at an event, or who has made an enquiry via your website. You want to move your business forward and you need to be able to make more calls with more confidence, but every time you go to pick the phone up there always seems to be something more attractive to be doing. You keep putting it off and you feel bad about it. You can't seem to overcome the anxious feelings that you associate with making sales and marketing calls. Occasionally you may call someone, they're not in, or you are told that they won't speak with you, or they do speak with you and you don't feel like you are getting anywhere on the call so you bring it to an end and breathe a sigh of relief. You want and need more confidence when it comes to speaking with people on the phone. After all, you're running a business and you have a lot riding on your success. You are carrying out different types of marketing but your budget is tight. The mail shots are working to a degree but not enough enquiries are coming in. Your social media profile is building nicely but you understand and accept that social media is all about building relationships, brand, visibility which of course takes time. In the same way, you are going to networking events but understand that networking and anything tangible that does come from your meetings is likely to take a while to come to fruition because again, networking is a superb business building activity but is based around building relationships over time with people and really should be more about what you can do to help others rather than "what's in it for me". That said, part of networking is being able to call people you have met at afterwards, and if you lack the confidence to do that then you've got to question how effective spending the time at the event was in the first place. Your website looks great but you have a vague feeling that you don't really know what it's doing for you. Is this sounding familiar? To many of you it will do, because I've met you, maybe not you specifically, but many, many small business owners like you. Interestingly, someone once told me that in a poll they read of biggest fears in business, cold calling came only second to speaking in public. If you're interested to know what came third it's quite an eye opener, it was dying! Even further down the list were things like flying, spiders, money problems, dogs etc.

Please relax. You are not alone, and this book will give you all the confidence and tools of the trade that you'll ever need to say goodbye forever to any concerns you have about using the phone as a business building tool. You'll be able to lose your phone fear and start finding more customers. You'll be able to call anyone, anytime, and have the confidence to effectively speak with potential customers in a natural comfortable way, not an uncomfortable rigid sales robot way. Not only that but you'll be able to cope with whatever comes your way, that's a promise, and don't worry I'm not going to ask you to turn into a super slick salesperson, that's the last thing you and your potential customers will want you to be. I'm on your side and here to help. Make absolutely no mistake about it, your telephone can be your most cost effective and lucrative marketing tool bar none.

So why would you want to be able to become great at making sales and marketing calls? Well, if you are in business, whatever type of business you might think you're in, I'd like to suggest to you that actually everyone is in the same kind of business. That business is the business of sales and marketing. That's it. You are in the sales and marketing business. End of story. If you don't believe that then why is it that in any given poll about the top reasons for small business failures is lack of sales given as being one of the major factors? Of course, a business coach will tell you and rightly so that planning, focus, organisational strategy, positioning, managing your time, your staff, are all important, and they are, an accountant will tell you that you need to keep a good eye on the numbers, and you do, an HR and health and safety consultant will tell you that you need to keep a close eye on your policies and compliance, and you do (there's a lot to running a business isn't there!) BUT here's the thing, none of that is remotely relevant if your till isn't ringing so to speak, if you're not actually making sales and doing business with real live customers and putting money in your bank account. Without making sales and carrying on making sales your business will sink. Sorry to be blunt about it but I'm here to help and be frank and open with you. No sales, no business, end of, full stop. You need to be doing as many different things as you can to put new leads into your pipeline, sales funnel whatever you want to call it. Websites, e broadcast, direct mail, social media, events, exhibitions, leaflets, sales letters, seminars, you name it, do it, all of these activities are hugely important. I'm not saying that the telephone is the golden bullet that can transform your business overnight, but what I'm really saying is that there is a place for picking the phone up in every business as part of, and there's the key, as part of your overall business development plan.

Maybe you are already an experienced salesperson and clearly understand the importance of the phone as an invaluable part of the sales process, but are looking for fresh inspiration to make your outbound calls more effectively. Well, there's plenty in this book for you too, particularly if you've been in sales a long time and find that the way you were originally trained to make calls just isn't working for you anymore. You maybe feel a bit worn out and want to draw a line in the sand and do something different. I can help. Interestingly I've worked over the years with many fantastic sales people who in a face to face environment are brilliant, but they'll openly admit that there's something about the phone that they just feel uneasy about. They prefer other people to make the calls for them which is fine if your Company have employed a separate team of in house telemarketers, or have allocated some of the marketing budget to outsource the calls to a telemarketing Company (I know a good one by the way!), but what if the buck stops with you to make your own calls, set your own appointments. You've got three choices really, one is get good at it, the others are avoid doing it, or do it poorly and not earn what you're capable of earning.

Believe me, the phone can be one of your most powerful and lucrative marketing tools but you're going to have to be prepared to completely shift the way you're thinking on this, to change the way you're talking to yourself about making calls, or cold calling, following up, telemarketing, telesales whatever you want to call it.

So here's the deal, I'll give you a no holds barred insight into how you make the phone work for you, if you keep an open mind and push your comfort zone enough to stick with me, and put what you're going to learn here into practice I promise you it will be one of the most valuable books you've ever read. Now that's a big claim I know, but it's true. Think about one of your best customers in terms of annual revenue to your business. Take that number and times it by the number of years your customers stay with you. Everyone's numbers will be different of course, but now picture in your mind the monetary figure of additional sales revenue over the lifetime of that one customer relationship and ask yourself if this book can help you to win even just one more customer like that (and it will do a lot more than that I promise you) is it worth your time in reading it? I'm going to give examples in this book where cold calls I've personally made have led to literally hundreds of thousands of pounds of revenue. Yes, that's right hundreds of thousands of pounds all from a "cold call" To the sceptics who say that it's impossible to win business of this magnitude over the phone, I say you're welcome to your opinion but you may well just be discounting one of the most sophisticated and powerful tools that you have at your disposal in your business, and its sitting on your desk, the telephone. Here's the point, despite increases in the complexity of technology, business people still respond very positively to a well thought out natural phone call. It has been said that some people in this technological world are actually losing the ability to communicate. Therefore those people in business who can get comfortable with communication in person with their target market on the telephone are going to be at a big advantage over those who can't. A lot of people who criticise telemarketing are actually people who don't have the confidence to do it. They are confident in giving opinions but give them a handset and a number to dial and they'll find something else to do. They prefer to sit on the sidelines and find excuses for why they are not calling people. For a second, let's put to one side cold calling and think about warm leads that have been generated via other marketing methods, networking, social media or events for example. At some point there will have to be a personal interaction, although there are some exceptions to the rule, for most businesses at some point in their sales cycle someone will actually have to pick the phone up and speak with someone. It can't all be done at arm's length. So again if you can become one of the people who can follow up with your leads in a natural easy way, you'll be ahead of those whose communication and systems online may be great but when it comes to actually speaking with someone they get anxious about it and maybe the sales process stalls because the person they are speaking with senses that the caller isn't exactly comfortable or doesn't appear confident in what they are talking about. Remember as someone once said. "Perception is reality" You may know your product/service inside out and upside down but if you can't convey that in conversation your potential customers may struggle to see the benefits of what you have to offer. Confidence is King.

So, you should want to become great at making sales and marketing calls because it will give you the edge, a competitive advantage, it will make you money.

The other important thing that differentiates using the telephone from any other form of marketing is that when you put the phone down after a conversation you pretty much know exactly where you stand with someone. With other forms of marketing often it can be quite some time before you get a sense of anything tangible in terms of feedback or direct results which can be frustrating. There's perhaps a feeling that you're not really sure what the effect of your efforts has been or will be, whereas with a phone conversation it is the most direct method of communication there is (apart from perhaps a face to face meeting, but more often than not it is a phone conversation that must take place in order to get the meeting in the first place!)

In fact, there are only 3 potential outcomes to that conversation:

1. The person you are speaking with absolutely is in the market for what you offer, and the next step of a meeting, a proposal, or an agreement to talk further after some initial information has gone over to them just makes sense to both of you. Believe me, if you make enough calls in the right way this is a very common outcome.

2. The person you are speaking with makes it clear that that, no, they are absolutely not in the market for what you have to offer. This is a positive outcome because you have now quickly established exactly where you stand with this particular prospect and can move on.

3. You both decide that whilst there isn't anything right now you can help with there is sufficient common ground for you to keep in touch to discuss future opportunities.

So, making outbound sales and marketing calls is an easy activity to test and measure, For any given time period you spend calling contacts, at the end of it you'll know exactly, how many calls you made, how many conversations you had, and from that how many appointments you set or qualified leads you uncovered for future progression. More of this in a later section, but obviously the natural progression from here is that when you attend those meetings and follow up with those leads it will be easy for you to measure your conversion ratios, and therefore be able to accurately establish how much revenue you generate at what profit margin. After a while you'll be able to predict the future, you'll know that if you or a member of your team make x calls, you'll generate y appointments and z leads, from which you'll have a predicted conversion ratio.

Remember the Pneumonic:

C A L (L) S

C   calls and conversations

A   automatically

L (L)   lead to

S   sales

Whatever your situation, I can help.

Remember though that for things to change, you've got to be prepared to do things differently, otherwise they'll just stay the same. The definition of madness is doing the same thing over and over again expecting a different outcome.

I saw this written on a poster, I'm not sure of the author but I think the words are superb. "To achieve an out of the ordinary success, your desire must be greater than the barriers you will have to overcome to achieve it." No doubt, in your quest to master the art of making sales and marketing calls there will be barriers, but make sure that YOUR desire is always higher than any barrier you face.

There's one other thing that I wanted to say about telemarketing before we start. There are as many opinions on how to make sales and marketing calls as there are stars in the sky. You've only got to Google the subject and you'll be bombarded with information from a myriad of people saying, do this, do that, don't do this, don't say that, use this technique or that technique, literally thousands of different articles on how to do this. In part, it's this overload of "how to" information that can create paralysis by analysis when it comes to sales. Whilst you will learn something from every article you read, everyone who has taken the time to put together some material on the subject has something valid to say, often coming from very different viewpoints but when you boil it all down the fact is if you're not making calls right now in your business and from tomorrow you started to, regardless within reason of what you said, or how you went about it I promise you that if you did enough of it consistently you'd end up generating positive outcomes, appointments, leads and sales. In my years working in sales I've developed my own take on what works and what doesn't. I've been trained by some well known Corporate Blue Chips, read the books, listened to the tapes and been on the seminars in my own quest to learn as much about the industry I work in as I can. Nothing however has taught me more than actually "doing it", making the calls, the good ones, the not so good ones, the great outcomes, and those calls where I didn't even get to base one.

It may be controversial for me to say that it doesn't really matter how you do it, but it's the truth. Above all it's about the action you choose or choose not to take. Yes, I'm going to give you everything you need based on my experience to make great sales and marketing calls, but even if you didn't read the book and all you did was to start picking your phone up and talking to people about your business, you'd sell a hell of a lot more than you are doing right now. That's because fundamentally it's not about this technique or that technique, using this phraseology or that phraseology, it's actually 90% about getting your head straight enough to pick your phone up in the first place. It's about **Maximising Your Phone Confidence™**

Now, of course I want you to read my book (I've burnt the candle late into the night to write it!) because it will help you with the mental game and also give you the practical tools to get started too, but don't let anyone kid you that you can't pick up your phone and start making calls before you've studied the subject inside out upside down first. That is the talk of the procrastinator. Everyone has a choice as to whether we let the procrastinator in us to triumph over what we know we should be doing.

I like the slogan of a well know sportswear brand. It could well have been written referring to making sales and marketing calls with the phrase "Just do it."

Look at this book as a Quick Start Guide. Once you're over your fears and concerns about picking the phone up and making calls has become a daily activity for you, there is plenty of scope to study the subject in more depth, such as advanced concepts and ideas about engaging people on the phone. For now though you just need to get started.

How to use this book

This book is designed to give you a solid basic introduction enabling you to build quickly to a point where daily telephone prospecting becomes comfortable, fun and above all productive.

This book is split into three parts. In part one I'll explain to you the psychology behind making sales calls from the point of view of the person making the call and also from the perspective of the person receiving the call.

In parts two and three I outline my **Straightforward Approach™** system. As the name suggests it is intentionally very straightforward. It is straightforward for you because it's an easy to follow set of steps that will have you up and running quickly making really effective calls for your business. Importantly though, it's also very straightforward for the people that you are going to be calling. They will know right up front what the call is about and importantly why that may be something they'll want to talk to you further about (or not). Either way, everyone knows where they stand and you can't be more straightforward than that.

Part two deals with the all important preparation you need to go through before you hit the phone. I'll show you different ways to reach your decision maker, alternative styles and call plans or call frameworks within which to structure your call and engage the person you're calling. I'll show you ways to develop and deepen the conversation to uncover information that will help you to match the benefits of your product/service to the specific situation of the person you're speaking with.

In part three, I'll help you with the dreaded "O" word, objections and why you have absolutely nothing to worry about. I'll give you the tools you need to deal with various common objections, as well as other things that can happen on a call which if not addressed can reduce your chances of a successful outcome. I'll also show you how to set quality appointments, develop sales leads that will add value and depth to your sales pipeline, and also how to agree next steps with the person you're calling so that things are not left "up in the air". Finally in this part I'll explain how to accurately track the progress of your calling and give you your very own personal action plan. Remember knowledge without action is just knowledge. It's the action that will determine your success, not just knowing what to do or say. I'll also be showing you ways to make yourself accountable and to be able to consistently and accurately test and measure your progress and results.

To get the most from the book I suggest that to begin with you first read it cover to cover. However, when you're reading have a big bold highlighter pen in your hand. I want you to interact with what you're reading, the book isn't designed to be read and then kept on a book shelf in pristine condition. However great it may be this book is never going to be a vintage works that can make you a few quid in the future or be the highlight of Antiques Road Show ("Oh yes, a fine example of How to **Maximise Your Phone Confidence™** by Robbie Stepney") It's designed for you to get involved, for you to keep it near your telephone so that when you're looking for guidance, inspiration and just pure courage before making some calls or when you're finding things tough you can dip back into it and re read the things that really struck a chord with you first time around. That's the point of the highlighter. Mark up any words, sentences, paragraphs that really work for you, things that inspire you, motivate you, or force you into action. My hope is that over time your book becomes dog eared, stained with coffee, ripped and generally very well worn because that way I'll know you've been using it. Don't stick it on a shelf because that's shelf development, not self-development.

Once you've read it once, go back through it again reading a few pages a day over a period of a month.

Scribble notes at the top and bottom of pages, take key phrases from it and put them up on your wall, do whatever it takes to absorb the information.

Then as I say, keep it on your desk near your phone, dip into it frequently, after a while you'll only need to look at it and the key messages/points from the book will come into your mind. I think NLP people call that an anchor, that's it, looking at the book will become an anchor for you. You'll look at it and start to get a feeling about making your calls, a confident, relaxed, un pressured feeling, a feeling that actually you're ok with speaking to anybody because every call has a positive outcome.

A word of warning though. It doesn't matter how many times you read this book, how many notes you make, how much you agree with the message, the content, the philosophy, the psychology, NOTHING will happen if you don't take action. Taking action is the key to everything. I have intentionally repeated this throughout the book because it is the only game in town. Action will get you to where you want to go. Inaction will kill your business.

Part One:

The mental game

Chapter 1

What are you thinking?

I don't put myself out there as being someone who has studied psychology, NLP, or behavioural science, in fact although I went to a cracking school, if I'm honest with myself I wasn't the greatest student and didn't make the most of the opportunities that were there for me. (Except for on the sports field but that's another story!) One thing however I know for sure is that when it comes to making sales calls all of us will perform in a certain way dependent on how we are thinking about it. That may sound simple but believe me all of us at times are great at coming up with reasons why we can't do something. Mark Rhodes in his book Think Your Way To Success says that the word "can't" actually means "won't" It's not that people "can't" pick the phone up to call potential customers it's that they "won't" They won't because before they even get as far as picking up the receiver they are creating as many reasons as they can why they won't do it right now. They know it makes sense, but they won't do it because of what's going on in their heads.

Let's be honest about it, if you knew that every call you made would end up in a positive outcome, namely you were going to set an appointment, generate a lead or even just have a good conversation, would you have any problem at all with picking the phone up? Of course not, that would be silly. So, it's the thought of what might happen on the calls in between the good ones that causes the anxiety.

Another way you can look at it is like this. If for every 100 dials of your telephone you knew that you would bring on board a new customer that was worth £1000.00 in revenue to your business, you could say that each dial of your phone is worth £10.00. If I promised to give you a crisp brand new £10.00 note for every cold call you made each day would you make them? Yes, you would because when you look at it in those terms I've reframed the outcome for you and you're focussing on the £10.00 per dial, and not the "I've got to make 100 cold calls"

Problem is that although the type of equation I've outlined above would hold true for everyone's business if we analysed it, with some of the numbers being quite unbelievable in terms of what the calls are worth to them on a pay per dial basis, it isn't how people view the activity of cold calling. It's human nature to focus on the anxiety of the unknown and the perceived problems that will be encountered when making the calls. That's why you and many other people just avoid making them. The rejection factor is dealt with in more detail below but it's a human fact of life that none of us like to feel like we're being rejected and so will avoid it all costs.

Here is a bit of fun with a list of some of the reasons why people won't pick up the telephone instead choosing to distract themselves with things that on the face of it need to get done but actually if they're honest with themselves don't need to be done now, or maybe not at all.

- Do the accounts
- Tidy the cupboards in the office
- Put the new wall planner up in the office
- Plan next week's plan.
- Purge/Back up e mail
- Surf the internet
- Get back late from lunch
- Go early to lunch
- Take the day off

- Attend a seminar about business development but then not take action
- Take the dog to the vet
- Go to the dentist
- Go somewhere else
- Have a meeting about something that really doesn't need one
- Re design their business cards for the third time
- Fill in their Outlook calendar
- Daydream
- Make another coffee
- Go and get a biscuit
- Spend hours pulling together a list of people to call (but then not calling them)
- Allow themselves to be distracted by endless interruptions
- Hard drive needs defragging (someone actually told me this once)
- Spend hours and hours on social media networks without having a purpose

A bit of fun as I say and I could have gone on forever but you're hopefully getting the message here that if you are absolutely adamant that there is something better to do than pick the phone up to talk with a potential customer then you will find that something. It's human nature, if you don't want to do something for any reason you'll start justifying to yourself why there is something better to do. We can all be great at convincing ourselves that what we've chosen to spend our time doing is going to be the most productive use of our time, even when we know 100% for sure it isn't.

So what's going on? The thought process you're going through in your mind all the time without you even knowing is dictating what actions you take.

THOUGHTS about a particular activity or situation lead you to **FEEL** a certain way about the activity or situation, which in turn will dictate the **ACTION** you take and the **RESULTS** you get.

- Thoughts
- Feelings
- Actions
- Results

So when you decide whether or not to do something you're basing that decision purely and simply on what is going on between your ears. The interesting part here is that you can have complete control if you want over that process to ensure positive outcomes but most people don't even realise that the process is taking place. If you think and then feel negatively towards something that's all you need to know, and because you think and feel that way you simply don't take the action. Brian Tracy, the hugely successful entrepreneur, speaker and author says in his bestselling audio programme The Psychology of Success that "Successful people do what they know they should do, when they know they should do it, regardless of whether they want to do it or not." So on that basis you know that you should be picking up the phone more to talk with potential clients, and to be frank until such times as you become really comfortable with doing it, you owe it to yourself and your business to "do it anyway" until you are.

The main problem here is the way in which you think about the activity of calling someone you don't know, and that is the root of everything. Let's have a look at some of the reasons business people I've met have given me for not wanting to get on the telephone with my thoughts in brackets on that reason.

- They won't be there (predicting an outcome before it's even happened, they may well be there, how do you know if you don't call?)

- They won't want to talk with me (maybe not, but equally they might want to and you aren't giving them the chance by not calling them)

- They'll be busy (in which case ok, they might not take the call, or may ask you to call back later so what's the problem there?)

- I won't know what to say (we'll get into call planning later but a good start point is Hello!-After all, you're calling about something you should know about really well, your business, but actually even more importantly and here's a clue for a later chapter, you should know really well what kinds of problems your potential customer may be facing that your product or service can solve)

- They might be difficult to talk to (they might be really easy to talk to)

- They might be annoyed that I've called them (they might just have been speaking about finding a solution just like yours two seconds before you called them)

- They might be rude or abrupt or just difficult (ok, they might be but equally they may be actually really nice and conversational and easy to speak with)

- No one likes getting calls (some people don't but plenty of people do)

- I don't like getting calls myself and I worry about what people will be thinking of me when I call them (you may not like getting calls because the type of calls you're used to getting are not that great, but after you've read this book the calls you'll be making will be great so why worry about what people are thinking. They may be thinking that they wish they had the confidence to make calls too. It's not calls people object to, it's bad, irrelevant calls and you won't be making any of those)

- The morning's not a great time to call (Millions of pounds worth of business is conducted every day in the UK on telephone calls made in the morning. Equally, thousands of sales appointments are set every day before lunchtime)

- The afternoon's not a great time to call (I think you know my answer to that one)

- Mondays and Fridays are not good days to call (every day of the week is a good day to call. Why eliminate 40% of your potential calling time on some kind of perception that no one talks to anyone on a Monday or a Friday)

- Mid-week people are busy (everyone in business is busy all of the time, part of their time is spent finding solutions to problems and issues they have in their business. Problems and issues that you may well have the solution to)

So, as we can see for every reason someone can put forward for being a good reason not to pick the phone up and call a potential customer it's not difficult to counter it with an equally compelling answer as to why the apparent hurdle in fact isn't even worth worrying about.

I don't want to get too heavy with this but there has been a shift recently towards the recommendation of cognitive behavioral therapy as a really successful treatment for people with illnesses like depression where the way a person is thinking affects them to such a point where they can't even function or have the motivation to complete even the most basic of tasks. CBT helps people to understand that it isn't events that happen to us that make us feel the way we do, it's how we interpret those events in our mind that in turn makes us feel a particular way about them and if we can change the way we think then those events will not trigger us into a negative way of thinking.

The far more ancient philosophy of Buddhism also helps us to understand how powerful our thoughts are. Buddhists believe that the root of all our anxiety about certain things we do or might want to do or situations we encounter comes simply from the meaning or attachment that we have in our mind to that situation or act. They teach us that if we can let go of all of that we can just be in the moment and our mind can be calmer in any situation.

I think Buddhists would make superb cold callers, calm, relaxed, focused and totally in the moment, without any pre conceived ideas or expectations on outcomes.

I guess what I'm saying here is that there is something that lies at the root of all of the above reasons people put forward as to why they can't/don't want to make calls and why the activity makes them feel the way they it does, and that's the fear of rejection.

Chapter 2

Dealing with rejection

When I go out speaking at business events I'll often ask the audience to put their hand up if they like making outbound calls. Not surprisingly there aren't many hands in the air, I then ask what is the main reason that stops them, and without a shadow of a doubt the overwhelming most positive response to that question is "Fear of rejection" The fear of rejection stops more people in business doing more things than anything else, and that is universally the case when it comes to picking the phone up.

It's human nature not to want to be rejected, we all want to be wanted This can come from all sorts of past experiences maybe even going back to childhood where we always sought our parents approval and felt bad when we didn't get it (There I go again, I'll get the couch out in a minute!) Your fear and worry of rejection may also be as a result of a bad previous experience of something totally unrelated to the activity that you are now avoiding because you just don't want to get that "rejected" feeling. It could have been that in the past you've asked someone out on a date and got turned down. Obviously an example I had first-hand experience of! Or it could be that you have had a previously bad experience of the actual activity you are avoiding. So maybe in the past you've made a call to a contact, were given a bit of a frosty response, felt uncomfortable and so now when you think about making another call you remember that feeling and it sends you into avoidance mode using any excuse you can not to do the activity.

The point is that it's the fear, concern, worry about rejection that is holding you back from making the calls you know you should be making for your business.

The sub tag line for this book is How To Lose Your Phone Fear and Win New Customers.

There's no point in me giving you 30 years' worth of practical tools tips and ideas on how to talk to people effectively on the phone if I haven't first dealt with any fear of rejection that you may have. Otherwise, you'll read the book, say yeah that sounds great Rob, but it's ok for you, you've been doing it for years, I can't because I still worry about rejection and what people are going to think, say, do etc.

Right, so here it is:

Rejection is not real. It does not exist. It ONLY exists in your mind, you create it, it is not tangible, it's a barrier that you put there purely because of the way you are thinking about your calls, and more importantly what you think you have got to "make happen" on the call. In your mind if you do not achieve the outcome you want from the call you have been rejected.

I'll say it again. Rejection is not real. It does not exist. It ONLY exists in your mind, you create it, it is not tangible, it's a barrier that you put there purely because of the way you are thinking about your calls.

Let me explain more.

Whenever you call a friend or someone you know really well, I think I'm on safe ground to say that you won't ever worry about being rejected. You don't get sweaty palms, a racing heart rate and that awful uncomfortable feeling. Someone I met recently explained it to me that when they see the list of people they have got to call they literally get a horrible sickness type feeling in the pit of their stomach. In all other areas of the private and business life they feel in complete control, never nervous, and actually on occasions they speak to large audiences but there's just something about the phone that makes them feel really bad. So what's going on, and why do people feel so differently when they have to call someone they don't know versus someone they do.

Level of Expectation and Being Someone Else

The difference is simply this. When you call a friend or someone we know really well, you have no pre conceived ideas about what the outcome of that conversation must be. You are completely relaxed and you just go with the flow. You don't try at any point to push an agenda or force a particular outcome, you just let the conversation unfold naturally. You talk a bit, they talk a bit, you ask some questions, they ask some questions and then you both know when that conversation has reached its natural (and natural) is the word here, conclusion.

However, when you pick up the phone to talk with someone in business you are probably feeling an overwhelming pressure (a pressure that is self-inflicted) to become someone else. You change your voice, maybe your accent, tone, volume, or speed of talking. The reason for this is that you feel like you now have to become "The Salesperson" Almost like an alter ego. You feel that the mission of your alter ego is to make it happen. Make the sale, set the appointment, generate the lead, gain commitment on this or that point, show the other person just how knowledgeable you are about your product or service. Problem with this is that all this expectation does nothing other than place an enormous amount of pressure on your shoulders before you've even dialed a number. You start to worry about the person you are calling not wanting to buy, to meet, to agree or commit to anything, so then the fear of rejection kicks in and all in all it's not a great place to be in mentally before you make a call. You are far from being relaxed, in fact you are in quite a high state of anxiety, the flight or fight mechanism kicks in. Then, laden with this pressure you call people, the tension and level of expectation and urgency in your voice is transferred down the telephone line to the other person. The other person picks up on this and so behaves in a particular way too (more of that in the next section) The conversation is quite awkward, stilted, doesn't flow, you are both feeling an uneasiness about the situation and so the call is brought to an end with neither person really gaining anything from it. You put the phone down, initially feel relief the call is over, but then the whole process of psychological build up starts again for the next call. No wonder with this kind of dynamic at work on the calls do so many people in business say that they really don't like picking up the phone. It is such a hard way mentally to go about it, and exhausting to put you through it like that on every call...and it's all self-inflicted.

Over the years I've worked in sales offices where people have arrived for work at 8.45am on day one in a role as an outbound telemarketer/salesperson and by 2.30pm they are destroyed mentally, literally that quickly. They are picking their coat up and are out the door. They just can't do it anymore. The pressure (actually the perceived pressure on their part but also sometimes the pressure put on them by others has got to them.)

So it's the way you are thinking about how you believe you have got to be or come across on the call that can make you feel so uncomfortable about it.

Remember that people you call will warm to you for the real you, not because you are being some kind of cardboard cut-out salesperson character. People are also very perceptive on the phone, they will absolutely pick up straight away if you are not being genuine.

More on this later, but for now just understand that you don't need to load this pressure on yourself, there is a much better way, an easier way, a more productive way, and I'll in later parts of this book be showing you how, step by step.

I mentioned earlier in this section the part CBT (cognitive behavioral therapy) can play in helping people to think differently. I'd like to give you brief overview of how some self-help CBT can assist you in overcoming your fears and negative feelings about the activity of calling people. CBT is a huge topic and I make no attempt here to give anything other than the briefest of insights into how one of the many techniques associated with the therapy can work in the context of cold calling. If however, the thought of delving deeper into the subject appeals, grab yourself a copy of CBT for Dummies by Rob Willson and Rhena Branch, it's a great practical read. Whilst you are at it, grab yourself a copy of two other books from the same publisher written by Mark Rhodes who kindly wrote the foreword to this book. The first is Think Your Way to Success, and the second How to Talk to Absolutely Anyone. The content of both books will help you massively in the area of improving your all round mindset and communication skills.

The basic model of CBT that outlines how to literally stop negative thinking in its tracks is shown below:

A- ACTIVATING EVENT-Start with recognising an activating event, in this case the event is that you know you have some sales calls to make.

B-BELIEFS-Now acknowledge your strongly held beliefs about the activity which begin to make you think in a certain way about making the calls. The thoughts make you feel a certain way, you start feeling nervous, anxious, begin avoidance behaviour, finding anything else to do rather than make the calls.

C-CONSEQUENCES Realise that there are consequences to the way you are thinking. You won't make the calls because of the thoughts going round in your head, and that in turn makes you feel even worse because you become very critical of yourself "I should have made the calls" "I'll never be able to get over this"

The above process all takes place very quickly in your mind, and simply makes it harder and harder for you to make the calls next time around when the whole process of negative thought patterns will start again.

So here's how CBT can help you to find another way to think about the activity...

D- DISPUTE Literally stop your negative thinking in its tracks by disputing what you are thinking. Ask yourself, what is the evidence that all the negative scenarios I'm conjuring up in my mind are actually going to happen? Most of the time you'll find that you jump to conclusions about potential outcomes, you become a mind reader seeing the future before it even happens. A lot of the time you will only see catastrophic events making them to be far more scary or unsuccessful, or difficult than they ever could be in "real life" By disputing what you're thinking you can put a stop to the negative thought patterns as soon as they arise and start to become debilitating to the point that they stop you taking action. So, if you start to think negatively about your calls stop doing it and dispute what you're thinking. Do not take things at face value, ask yourself, seriously is that true? Would that really happen? Honestly what are the odds of the person saying that, doing that, being like that?

E-EXAMPLES-Finally, now you've stopped the negative thought pattern with the ABCD method above write down as many counter arguments as you can to the way you've been thinking. For example you may have been thinking, "no one will want to talk to me" You've then disputed with "hang on a minute, is that genuinely true that NO ONE will want to talk to me?" Now to well and truly kick this negative thought about your calls where it hurts you may come up with the following examples of an alternative viewpoint "well, ok maybe some people won't want to take my call, but there will be plenty that will" "ok, so I might not set an appointment on my first call with this person, but as I've read Robbie Stepney's How to **Maximise Your Phone Confidence™** I'm ok with that and realise that my calls are not "do or die" they are simply an additional marketing method for my business that I'm going to approach in a relaxed way, and I'm ok with the outcome, whatever way it goes"

Once more, it's the quality of what you're thinking that is the biggest deciding factor in how successful you'll be at any given task, in this case making sales calls. To be frank anything else is secondary, if you can't get your head straight nothing else will help you. Read all the books you like, listen to all the tapes you can, but if your head is all over the place none of that will help you.

I have over the years worked with many people in sales offices who have been very accomplished telemarketers who have been real assets to their companies. They often have an easy way about them that people warm to and also have the very valuable ability to use humour at appropriate times to build rapport with people, and quickly gain common ground. Often though as I got to know them better it became clear that in their minds however they saw themselves more as solid telemarketers able to develop high quality sales leads as opposed to being someone who was able to just go that step further and set lots of sales appointments and to secure dates in the diary. I was able to help a lot of these people to see that the only barrier stopping them from setting more sales appointments was the one they had put in their own mind about it. We looked at their belief and using the ABCDE model we were able to help them see that logically there was no evidence whatsoever to suggest that they could not set more sales appointments. After all, they were already having excellent quality conversations with people so the only thing missing was their belief that at the appropriate time in the call they could move it along to an appointment. I would talk with them about this and offer some good ways that they could do it (and you'll be learning them later too) and from that moment on almost overnight they became appointment setting machines, right up there with the best of the best in the Company. It was fantastic to see their confidence soar, which naturally led to them becoming even more accomplished as they felt better and better about what they were doing and their abilities. In reality although yes, we'd tweaked some words here and there, the fundamental change had all taken place in the mind.

Chapter 3

What are they thinking?

One of the things I enjoy most is asking business people what they think about the quality of the calls they receive in their office. I'll often do this when I'm speaking at an event. At first many people are a little bit tentative in letting me know what they really think. After all, they know that I run a telemarketing Company so probably think that they need to be a bit diplomatic. Usually someone will start with something quite generic like "Well Robbie, the quality varies" or someone will add "Don't really know enough about the subject to comment", so at that point I say "Right guys gloves off, you're not going to offend me because like you I receive some really bad calls in my office, in fact just last week..." I then tell them about a recent call I've received that has stuck in my mind for all the wrong reasons. Well, at that point the floodgates open! I can't stop people...one after another, after another, people standing up and ranting about telemarketing calls they receive and why they hated the call so much. It really is quite funny to see people let rip. Bottom line is that for most people in business cold calls have become something they've really got an aversion to. They really, really don't like them. So hang on Robbie, you've just spent the last few pages telling us that cold calling can be a really useful addition to our marketing plans, but now you're telling us that most business people don't like receiving them, make your mind up! Let me explain, it's not cold calls business people don't like, it's bad cold calls they don't like.

So, what are they kinds of things business people tell me they really don't like about the calls they receive. Let's have a look at the top 10 reasons in turn and examine why they can be such a turn off or hang up!

1. **Being Over Familiar/Not saying who they are, where they're from and the *real reason for the call*-** We've all had them, "Good morning Robbie, how are you today?" Problem here is not that people mind being asked how they are, well not by for example a wife, husband, good friend, work colleague etc, but there's something about someone you don't know asking you how you are that for us here in Britain that just well, kind of gets up our nose, it gets our back up before we even start. We straight away go on the defensive. The caller is asking how we are not because they are interested how we are but really as a way to in their mind to gain some common ground. Gaining common ground is a good thing, but this isn't the way to do it. The point is that regardless of how this question is answered the caller is just going to carry on with their agenda and we as people receiving the calls know that, so it's basically a pointless, false, unauthentic way to start a call. A lot of business people I speak with also tell me that they find it quite infuriating when people call them but don't quickly explain who they are, where they're from and what the **real** reason for the call is. I say **real** reason because a common complaint amongst people being called is that salespeople will often try and call under some kind of other guise to hide the real reason for their call. They almost try to creep up on someone by starting the conversation in one way and then revealing their true agenda. This does nothing other than to alienate people. Being straightforward wins friends, being

crafty and underhand is pointless and does nothing to promote the reputation of professional sales people.

2. **Not asking if it's a good time to talk-** Business people tell me that they find it very irritating when they get a call and the caller just launches into some kind of script (see below) without even checking if it's a good time to talk. Business people are all very busy and could be doing any one of a thousand different things when the phone rings. Some of those things will not stop them from continuing with a call but a lot will, so checking is a good idea. Some old school sales books will tell you to never ask if it's a good time to talk because you're giving the person an opportunity to say no. Point is, why would you want to speak with someone when it's not a god and convenient time to talk, it's not going to be a productive conversation. Isn't it better to simply arrange a better time to talk?

3. **Reading a script-** This is a big one, people hate feeling that they are having a script read at them. It just completely kills all chances of any kind of genuine natural conversation developing. There are people who have an ability to make a script sound more natural but even they can't get away from the fact it's a script and the person they're calling knows it. Sure, we need a call plan but not a script, throw it away. I call these kinds of rigidly scripted calls "Dalek calls" If you remember the Daleks from Doctor Who you'll see where I'm coming from here!

4. **Not listening-** People like to be listened to and understood. Too many salespeople ignore the well-known mantra of "You have two ears and one mouth, so use them in that ratio" I'd add to that my own one of "Shut up, listen and respond accordingly" People are turned off by salespeople who love the sound of their own voice and who don't listen. I had a friend who used to train sales people for estate agents. He

told me story once of when he did a field visit with one of the sales people on his team who was particularly guilty of not listening. They entered the house of an elderly lady who had asked for a valuation. As they did so the sales person said "So how are you Mrs. Jones?" to which the lady replied "Oh, not so good really, I've just lost my husband and that's why I need to sell the house, it's too big for me on my own" The sales person had not been listening, his focus was just on getting the instruction so instead of "responding accordingly" he replied "That's interesting, lovely garden, I bet you and your husband enjoy sitting out there" Enough said on that one, like I say, shut up, listen and respond accordingly.

5. **Being uninformed-**When you receive a call from someone who doesn't know what they're talking about they stand out a mile. They often try to fill their knowledge gaps by talking, and talking, and talking and giving hugely generic answers to any questions asked. You owe it to yourself to know your products or service inside out and upside down. Having great product knowledge will instill confidence ion the people you're talking about. As well as having great product knowledge, make sure you have great industry knowledge too. Read trade magazines, subscribe to groups and forums that cover your subject or industry on the internet.

6. **Being assumptive-** Sales people who assume that what they've got is absolutely spot on and right for everyone they call just annoy people. How is it possible to know whether what you have is right for someone if you haven't even had a conversation to find out more about their particular set of circumstances.

7. **Being overly enthusiastic-**This is an interesting one and may come as a bit of a surprise to anyone who has been on a traditional sales training course. We've all been told that

enthusiasm sells. It does, but only if it is authentic and at appropriate times. Over the top false enthusiasm especially right at the start of the call just switches people off. One lady at a talk I gave on telemarketing described this typical over the top enthusiasm as sounding like a local radio DJ voice.

8. **Being pushy or aggressive-** Straightforward this one, people like to buy, they don't like to feel that they are being forced to buy, pushed to buy, prodded to buy, manipulated to buy...you get the picture. They want to be helped to buy. Helping people to buy is very different to pushing people to buy. Salespeople need to understand that "no" does often mean "no" and isn't popular to common belief a green light to start putting the heat on, twisting people's arms, pressurising people into buying. "No" sometimes does not mean "no" but there are ways and means to find that out in a professional manner that we'll explore later in the book.

9. **Over promising and under delivering-** Salespeople will often tell people what they think they'll want to hear in order to win the business, rather than being completely open, frank and upfront about what their product/service can do for the customer. They make exaggerated claims which may help them close a deal in the short term but the fallout from that is once the claims are not substantiated as the product/service fails to deliver, the salesperson loses their credibility and crucially they've also lost the most valuable commodity they can have in a seller buyer relationship, and that's trust.

10. **Falling short on administration-** It's a common trait amongst many salespeople that they love the selling part, the thrill of the chase so to speak but once the sale is made they lose interest in the all-important after sale administration. There may be notes that need to be written

23

up following the phone conversation with a client that will help the order fulfillment team deal quickly with the customers' requirements or financial paperwork that needs to go through to the accounts team. Whatever it is, the feedback I hear from business people is often that what they were told on the phone call in terms of what would happen next when they agreed to move forward did not materialise and they were left frustrated with having to make calls themselves to find out what was happening with their order. This all goes towards them again having a negative view of the salesperson who called them.

So, there you are, the list doesn't make great reading and there were a few comments believe me that were unprintable.

The important point to remember here is that when the phone rings in the offices of the people you'll be calling many of them will be starting the conversation with the kinds of thoughts and observations in their minds I've listed above about what your call is going to be like. So, you need to be different, to show that your call isn't going to follow the stereotypical sales call route. Believe me, when you do, you'll find that people are more than happy to speak with you and whilst of course not everybody you call is going to become a customer you are guaranteed to have more genuine authentic conversations with people where everybody is being themselves.

I believe that many sales calls made in let's call it the traditional way are doomed from the start. Reason is that the salesperson is not being natural, they have their "sales head" on and the person being called isn't being natural either because they have their suit of armour on that's there to deflect and keep them safe from salespeople. End result is a superficial conversation that has little depth and is going nowhere fast.

As you'd expect, in the interests of balance I also ask people when I'm doing talks about telemarketing to give me some examples of calls that really stood out for all the right reasons, ones where they really enjoyed speaking with the sales person. It won't surprise you to know that the kinds of reasons they give for them thinking the call was a good one are the complete opposite of the poor qualities I've listed above. The call was good because:

1. The caller was friendly but in a professional way, and also very straightforward in their approach.

2. They checked if it was a good time to talk, in other words respected the person's time

3. The caller was natural in the words they used, the speed and tone of their voice, and were clearly not a Dalek! (rigidly scripted)

4. They listened and if they were unclear on anything they checked for clarification to make sure they'd understood correctly

5. They knew their stuff, were well informed about their product or service and also had clearly done their homework on the Company they were calling.

6. They never assumed at any point that the sale was in the bag.

7. They were positive but in an authentic way, not in an overly or falsely enthusiastic way.

8. There was no hint of being pushy or aggressive, or the use of overt "sales techniques" to move things forward.

9. In the instances where the call resulted in a sale, the product/service did what the sales person had said it would.

10. All requests for further information or the completion of after sale administration were dealt with efficiently.

It's not rocket science this is it!

So here's an exercise for you to do. I want you to think about the last time you received a call in your office. What did you like about the caller? What didn't you like? Did you feel your barriers going up quickly, and if so why was that, or were you happy to speak with the person, why was that? By analysing your own reactions to calls you've received or will receive from now on, you'll start to see the kinds of words, phrases, and tones of voice that almost subliminally force you to flick the "off switch" and make you want to bring the call to an end quickly. Equally, the good calls stand out, and a pattern will also emerge for the words, phrases and tones of voice that keep you engaged and happy to continue talking.

In the same way that I explained that often sales people are not authentic, people on the receiving end of sales calls, because of the way they perceive the call is going to go if they sense the salesperson is not being straightforward with them also become unauthentic. They will retreat, become defensive to protect themselves. What you end up with is two people neither of whom is being themselves, using words that are not theirs, wrapped up in personalities that have been fabricated to play their part in what often is nothing more than a pantomime.

Clearly, these interactions don't do anyone any good at all. I've often thought how much more business would be conducted so much quicker if everybody just dropped the facade and was just natural, authentic and real. The sub text of those conversations would go something like this. "Look I just want to know if ABC product/service is genuinely something you are happy to talk about, or are considering for your Company in either the short medium or longer term. If you are then great let's talk, and if not don't worry about me pressuring you into making you say something different, I'll just accept what you say and move on. Obviously if you have questions about what we do I'm happy to answer them, I've no agenda here other than just establishing where we both stand" Answers could range from," Thanks for being up front and straightforward, no, not something for us now or in the future," to" Yes, actually happy to talk about that because it is a product/service we're looking at/have considered looking at, can you tell me more, or "Can I tell you more about where we are with it, or "That might be something we're going to look at, let's talk about it" Time taken to establish where everyone stands 30 seconds. Problem is that these kinds of conversations are a million miles away from the pantomime I mentioned earlier. In the pantomime, unfortunately too many sales people talk absolute nonsense in an attempt to sneak up on the person they are calling. They will often cloak the real reason for the call behind some kind of smoke screen like surveys, you've been selected, I was referred to you by... They use these kinds of approaches because some bright spark somewhere has trained them to think that it's clever to manipulate the people they are calling. They look upon the list of people they have to call simply as numbers, a list of targets to be manipulated. They focus only on their own objective, the sale, the money. The reality though is that all they are doing by calling like that is alienating people and forcing those barriers up in double quick time. End result is that the person being called feels threatened they go into survival mode in an attempt to get away from the caller. They respond with things like I'm in a meeting can you call me back, call me next week, next month, next year, send me information, not a good time to talk right now. Alternatively they may just become quite blunt and to the point, even rude to get rid of the caller. They most probably are rarely blunt or rude to anyone in any other situation but that's the effect that sales calls can have on people.

So what's the answer? How do we get to a point where productive conversations for both caller and person being called can take place? In other words how do we stop the pantomime?

It's actually very easy, it's just about being very straightforward in your dealings with people, and on that basis there's a much higher chance that they'll be straightforward with you too.

Part Two:

Straightforward Approach™ The powerful telemarketing system guaranteed to get results!

Does what it says on the tin-an overview.

If you look up the word straightforward in any of the main English dictionaries you'll find the following definition for the adjective:

Not complicated to do, or to understand, easy to follow.

In relation to describing people as straightforward the dictionary offers the following definitions:

Open, honest, frank.

Put the word into a thesaurus and it gives you the following:

Direct, genuine, sincere, candid, forthright and up front.

So I've developed a system based on my considerable number of years holding a telephone in my hand that does what is says on the tin- above all it is straightforward.

For the people using the system it's not complicated to do, or to understand, and it's really easy to follow.
For the people who'll be receiving your calls, because you'll be adopting this system, they'll find you to be open, honest, frank, direct, genuine, candid, forthright, and above all up front.

Now, let me ask you a question. Does that sound like the kind of person who people will want to do business with?-YES! You will stand out a mile from your competition.

Believe me, the above definitions of the word straightforward are not I think you'll agree generally used to describe sales people, but they are absolutely essential characteristics that you'll need to adopt, display and live by if you want to maximise your sales opportunities on the telephone.

I've spent a lifetime studying how to develop business over the phone and in **Straightforward Approach™** I take the very best of what works, thrown away what doesn't, added a huge spoonful of over 20 years of experience of making calls and given you a system that I promise you if you use it and work at it you'll win more new business that you ever thought possible.

I'm not saying that this is a definitive guide to cold calling, telesales or telemarketing. As I said earlier in the book there are many different views and philosophies out there on how to make sales calls and it's a massive topic. What I am saying however is that it will give you a solid platform to get you over your nervousness and concerns about making calls, and importantly it works!

Once you start to win business by using these techniques you'll naturally want to develop your skill and knowledge in the subject and I can definitely help you with that too, but for now let's take the first step.

I can't be more straightforward than that.

Chapter 4

Organisation and tools
of the trade

We've all heard the expression the 6 P's, right? Well if not here they are below:

- Proper
- Prior
- Planning
- Prevents
- Poor
- Performance

To do anything successfully in life you have to have a plan. Without a plan you are like a yacht with no sail, boat without a rudder, car without a steering wheel, yes ok Rob we get it!

If you want to implement outbound calling to become a successful and lucrative part of your overall marketing activities you'll need to plan thoroughly. Don't worry if you're not a great planner because I'm going to give you in this section everything you need to do, in the order you need to do it. When I'm asked to go into companies to help them improve with their outbound calling one of the first things I ask them is what planning have you done to put in place a mapped out process for the activity. Often that question is met with a bit of a blank stare, or a response that indicates to me that actually not much thought has gone into the preparation phase, and it's been more a case of right we need to make some calls, Bill you can do it, grab a directory and start dialing! Whilst I'm all for taking action, it needs to be the right action with the right thought, preparation and planning otherwise the action is destined to either fail, or not be as effective as it could have been. So, where do you start? Easy, you need to become a sniper. Becoming a sniper means that your efforts will be focused in exactly the right place rather than diluted with a generic, wide approach.

The Sniper Checklist:

The Who

Who specifically do you want to be speaking with on the telephone to win more new business. In marketing circles they call this The Target Market. Put simply it's the group of people who based on your own knowledge and experience of your industry are most suited to and are most likely to have an interest in what you have to offer. By way of an example, if you're selling cold drinks on a beach, your target market is people who have been in the sun too long and have a mouth like the bottom of a budgies cage. The people who based on everything you know about them in principle you'll have the most common ground with. A poor example of a Target Market would be selling thick duffle coats on a market pitch in August. So how do we make sure we don't go home from our market with a boot load of duffle coats? If we could wave a magic wand and a list of ideal customers appears, what would they look like?

Here are some questions you will want to ask yourself:

What is the job title of the person most likely to evaluate and take decisions on your type of product/service?

What industry sectors are likely to be fertile ground for you?

How big are your ideal customers in terms of employee size, or turnover?

How many offices will they have, just one head office single site, or will they be companies likely to have branches?

Are there any industry sectors that you definitely don't want to target?

Are there any specific Companies that you don't want to target?

Is it important to you how long your target companies have been trading?

Are you looking to sell only to Limited Companies or all types of business set up?

The above questions are really important. It's easy to say, well we want to do business with everyone, but your approach will then be more scatter gun or blunderbust (what a great word) rather than sniper.

The Where

Geographically where is your target market located?

Do you want to be selling just locally, county wide, nationally, or internationally?

The Why

Once you've answered these questions ask yourself Why? Why have you given the answers that you have to the questions. Do your answers stack up in terms of looking at your current client base, or if you are a start up, do your answers make sense bearing in mind what the key benefits are that your product/service delivers? (More on benefits later)

A good way to test your Target Market assumptions is to put yourself in the shoes of the person you will be calling. If you were in a particular job role at a Company of a certain size involved in ABC industry with an office in ABC Town and you received a call from a Company looking to talk about XYZ product or service, does it make sense that you'd want to find out more. Would their call be well received by you and by that I mean would it be relevant to you?

If everything stacks up and makes sense to you then you have your Target Market.

Some people say to me that they find it difficult to pin down who exactly their ideal customers are. The good old flip chart, or a pad and a pen are good ways to brainstorm your ideas and then just tweak and tweak again until you get a profile that makes sense. I keep saying that to emphasise the point. Does it make sense to call these people? If there's any doubt in your mind then you need to get tweaking again.

Getting Your List Together

So, great, you've identified what your ideal customers look like, so now where do you go to get a list that matches your criteria? In my experience, this is where many people fall down in their preparation. Having put in the time to plan the Who, Where and Why they then go and grab the nearest Directory and start calling in a very ad hoc way. Their results are ad hoc too, but there's a whole list of reasons for you not to just go and pick up the nearest business Directory, or print off details from Directory websites, and one of them could cost you money.

Keeping It Legal

The Corporate Telephone Preference Service Register and its domestic version the TPS were set up a number of years ago by the Direct Marketing Association to enable Companies that no longer wish to receive telemarketing calls to register that wish. Anyone making outbound calls both B2B and B2C is required by the legislation to check any number they want to call against the latest versions of the registers which are updated every 28 days. Companies can be fined up to £5000 for breaching the legislation so it just makes sense to make sure you're on the right side of the legislation when planning your telemarketing activity.

You want to be able to call with confidence when dialing your numbers so you definitely don't want to have in the back of your mind a doubt as to whether the company you are calling is on the CTPS. Apart from anything else, why would you want to risk the first thing someone says to you being "We are on the CTPS, why are you calling us?" Not exactly the greatest start to a call and doesn't make you look too professional either.
For further information on the CTPS visit www.tpsonline.org.uk

The good news is that it is so easy to adhere to the rules and regulations as long as you buy your lists from approved data providers who will have pre screened the data for you before releasing it.

The Direct Marketing Association is a good port of call when looking to source data providers to talk to. There are lots of companies selling data and they are split into different camps. Some specialise in quite niche contact lists where as others are more generalist.

Speak to a few and let them know exactly what you need and they'll guide you through the process.

The DMA website is very informative on a whole range of issues relevant to helping businesses with their marketing and well worth a visit www.dma.org.uk

Data Licenses

Just a few points on data licenses. The list you buy will be licensed to you under one of three license agreements, namely single use, multi use, and what in the game is called eternal. Terms and conditions are always supplied with your data list. Single use as the name suggests means that your data contacts are licensed to be called just once, or one conversation (check with your data provider on their specific definition of what "once" is as it can be a grey area...like so many other things) Bottom line here though is that you have just the one shot so to speak. With a multi use list you can call your contacts typically up to 12 times in a 12 month period, after which time (as is the case with single use lists) the data should be (and here's a great word..see if you can get it into your next phone conversation) "expunged" from your IT systems. What that means in basic terms is that you have 12 months of working the list to identify those people with whom you have common ground and are interested in talking further with you, meeting you, buying from you, coming to your events etc. Obviously once you have gained someone's agreement that they are happy to have future contact from you then the CTPS is no longer in play as there is an existing relationship, which is common sense really. The eternal license means you have the contacts for life, you can call them as many times as you like for as long as you like to uncover opportunities from the data. Goes without saying that single use costs less that multi use which costs less than eternal. My personal view is that if you're buying data in sensible quantities and by that I mean you will have time to comfortably call and qualify the contacts within a 12 month period then it's questionable why you'd want an eternal license but that as they say is a matter for you. Speak with a data specialist and they will make sure you don't go too far wrong.

Please bear in mind that the CTPS/TPS registers are updated every 28 days. What that means is that you should be checking your numbers against the register to ensure your compliance every 28 days and eliminating those numbers which may have been placed on the register since your list purchase. Just because you have bought your data from a data provider it does not relieve you of the obligation to adhere to the code of conduct re outbound calling. Again the DMA website contains information on companies who can provide you with desktop applications to screen your lists against the latest versions of the TPS/CTPS. You just download some free software onto your desktop and then buy credits for numbers to be checked at a cost of approximately 1p per number so minimal cost for the peace of mind it brings.

All of the above is just common sense really, and for a little bit of homework and preparation you can make sure you are as I said earlier "Calling with confidence" The confidence in this case refers to the fact you know that you're spot on rte your contact data.

In the real world let's be frank about it, plenty of people will be calling from all sorts of sources like old paper directories, online directories, yearbooks magazines, etc. Problem here is that your data is likely to be inaccurate, and many directories strictly prohibit their use for marketing purposes. You're all grown up people but it's my job to point out to you the way this stuff works.

Data companies and directory publishers for example will sometimes put "seed contacts" on a list, otherwise known as "ghost companies" which means that for all intents and purposes the number looks like it belongs to a bona fide company but in reality the number calls through to their offices so they can see who is being naughty with their data.

At the end of the day I can (for those of you who like to skim read) sum up my previous 600 odd words with just three... buy decent data!

Some people say to me that they can't be bothered to source data this way and will just "pull together some contacts" Believe me that's just lazy and actually false economy. Any telemarketer worth their salt will tell you that "the money is in the list", and the better the quality of the list the more money you'll find in there. Also think about it this way. If you're selling a product or service which is worth over the lifetime of the customers relationship multi thousands of pounds, doesn't it just makes sense to spend a few quid putting a professional, well thought out contact list together which will pay you back handsomely.

If you were getting married you wouldn't take a chance by inviting just anyone to the bash in the evening would you? No, you'd know exactly who you want to invite and why. Well going after new business is exactly the same. Know who and why and then get some decent contacts together.

Without a doubt the section above will save you hours and hours of time. You will end up speaking to more people, quicker than if you try to find your contacts in any other way.

Data Costs

Ballpark figures at the time of writing would be about £300 per thousand but again varies according to whether the lists is a generalist one or niche, what additional information is given on the list over and above the basics and of course (for those of you who have been paying attention) whether its Single Multi or Eternal Use.

Knock your list into shape

Your list as we said will be supplied to you in an Excel sheet format. First thing to do is to save the original version to a secure back up area on your PC and then create a second version of it to on your desk top. This is going to be the version you are going to be working with. You'll be adding certain columns to it which will make your life considerably easier when it comes to rattling through your calls and maybe deleting some as well which may not be needed so let's have a look at what's involved. Here is a list of columns that you should have on every call list you work from and I suggest in this order too, although it really comes down to personal preference.

1) Company Name
2) Contact Name
3) Job Title
4) Industry Sector
5) Phone number
6) Call back date
7) Call back time
8) Call Notes
9) E mail address
10) Website Address
11) Address 1 (First part of address)
12) Address 2 (Second part of address)
13) Town
14) County
15) Postcode
16) Employee numbers on site*
17) Turnover*

*When you source your data the data company will be able to supply this information, and there are other criteria too that you can get if you really want it like how long the Company has been established etc. If you feel that your list has columns on it with information that you don't really want on your working copy then just delete them.

The Excel spreadsheet is the workhorse of telemarketing activity. It is not and never should be designed to be a place where you keep all your qualified accounts, prospects, leads, and opportunities. It is simply a tool to enable to quickly work through a large number of potential customers and uncover the gems.

If the Excel sheet is the workhorse then the CRM system is your thoroughbred.

CRM systems- having somewhere to keep the good stuff

This is the place you should be putting all the "good stuff" (technical term). The good stuff being people you've set appointments with, or had really good conversations with where agreement has been given that you can go back to the contact again at some point in the future (you'll see when we get into the nuts and bolts of calling that you should never leave something as loose as "we'll talk again at some point in the future" but for the purposes of lists I'm just making the point that if someone has had a deep enough conversation with you in order for you to have established common ground and gained their agreement to talk again, then it makes sense for you to treat that opportunity like gold dust and put it somewhere where you will never lose the details of the opportunity, the conversation, what was important to them, and any other key information. That place is a CRM system.

What is a CRM system? What does it do? and Why should you have one?

I am no expert on the intricacies of CRM systems, but that's ok because you don't need to be an expert either. There are as with everything plenty of experts who if you really want to will visit your business and give you the A-Z of any given system, but what I want to do here is give you the crash guide on the bits you need to know. After all the purpose of this book is to get you on the phone making phone calls to win business.

A CRM (Customer relationship management) system is quite simply software that enables you to manage your company's interactions with past, current and future customers all in one safe and secure place, easily accessible at anytime. You can record all relevant and useful information about any given customer far and above basics like name, address phone number, e mail, and also get the system to give you reminders when important call backs have been scheduled for you. The scope of all CRM systems enables to one degree or another help you to manage sales, marketing, customer service and even accounts functions. However for the purposes of this book I'm just concentrating on the sales side of things. The products vary in terms of being locally held on your PC or increasingly so many systems are now cloud based simply being accessed via a secure log in from your desk top. The functionality goes from being basic to advanced dependent on your requirements and most systems can grow with you, in other words you can start off having a system just for you or you and a couple of colleagues but if you need to add more users you can. Prices vary from free systems giving basic functionality through to varying monthly subscriptions typically taken out on an annual basis for a set number of users. The key point about CRM and this is why you should have it is that for many SME businesses they hold information especially regarding sales opportunities in many different places, often according to the personal preference of the people working there. In a hypothetical Company, Jim for example may be a bit old school and he only likes to write stuff down on a pad, or in an A4 diary or on the back of a fag packet. He hates technology and says that he can always find whatever he wants about a sales account or contact at the flick of a page. Problem is though that at his last sales appointment he left his diary on the roof of his car as he was organising his briefcase on the back seat and his state of the art sales contact system is now laying in the road somewhere. John meanwhile thinks Jim is an idiot. John keeps all his contacts "Up here" and he taps his head when he's telling you this. Problem is that although John has it "up there" no one else can see it or access it. Jane though has it all worked out. She uses Outlook reminders for when she needs to follow up with people, problem is that her Outlook calendar has just crashed and she's lost the lot. You see my point here. The information you will be uncovering from your calls is very, very valuable and you need a bullet proof, organised place to put it that everyone within your business can access. Reason for this is that more than one person in a business may have contact with a potential customer and if the details are not put somewhere where everyone can see the latest state of play then problems can arise. Hypothetical example: You uncover through your calling that Simon Davis the Facilities Manager of a Company may well be interested in what you have to offer. His colleague Jane is really helpful and has given you his direct line. However, she adds that under no circumstances should anyone call Simon before 9.30am in the morning. Your colleague in the office has seen that Simon Davis is currently a prospect and decides to follow up with him the next day as you are off ill. No problem with that, except that she calls Simon Davis at 9.15am. He isn't very happy and says, I was expecting your call but I know that you were told not to call me before 9.30am. Don't you talk to each other in your office? Result there is that an opportunity has been lost.

The importance of multi touch marketing and how CRM helps

We are all learning more these days about the importance of "multi touch" marketing, that is making contact with potential customers on a number of occasions in different ways in order to encourage them to do business with you. I've heard various numbers suggested as the average number of "touches" before a company makes a buying decision, (anything from 5-10) and that could be a combination of phone call, e mail, personal meeting, newsletter etc. Whatever the number I can tell without a shadow of a doubt that one touch will rarely do it for you. You are going to need to follow up with the people in your sales pipeline if you want to achieve any degree of success. That said it is also very common for people not to like following up, with only a small percentage making more than one attempt to re connect with a potential customer. That's mad isn't it? You're reading this book because you'd like some help with overcoming some of the barriers that may hold you back from picking up the telephone, so I have some good news for you. A follow up call is a walk in the park compared with making the first one, which by the way you will also think is a walk in the park, in the sunshine, once you've finished this book. So, all you need to be successful is a good system to help you manage your call backs and remind you when you need to be making them-a CRM system.

Some systems you may want to check out

I make no personal recommendation on CRM systems, I can tell you that within my businesses we use Salesforce because we like it, but there are plenty of decent systems out there. You may want to have a look at Act!, Zoho, Infusionsoft, Saleslogix and a bit of research on the web will throw up a few more candidates too.

Have a look, pick one and use it.

Pitfalls of CRM

A word of warning here. Your CRM system and what it can do for you will depend to a large degree on your discipline to use it. The old mantra of quality in, quality out applies here. You must put good quality notes into the system in order to give it a fighting chance of helping you. If you don't, it won't be able to and more importantly that will cost you opportunities, sales, revenue and success.

Do not under any circumstances be tempted to import bulk data lists into your CRM. It will just clog up your system if you do that. As I said before, work your lists to find the gems and then put the gems into your CRM. There are some bespoke telemarketing software systems that are purpose built for bulk import of contacts but to cover their use here would be going beyond the scope of the book. If you really want to look at something like that do some research and get someone to give you a demo. I'd suggest however that for the majority of people reading this a basic system will suffice.

Setting Up Mission Control-Your working environment

Ok so you now know how to work out the who, the why, where to get data from and what to do with the good stuff when you find it. We're now going to talk about setting yourself up for success, and by that I mean giving a lot of thought to the environment, the process, the schedule you set up for yourself as far as outbound calling is concerned.

You will have heard the saying "You are a product of your environment", and never has that been truer than when it comes to getting in the zone to pick the phone up. We looked earlier at all the different reasons why people can be distracted from making their sales calls. Take my word for it; if you don't put in place a regular regime and stick to it you are setting yourself up for a fall.

So, the where is the first important decision to make about your outbound calls and to a large extent will be dictated by your own personal situation. Are you for example working from home, from an office on your own, from a shared office, do you work from the car most of the time?

Let's look first of all at the home working environment which is where many people start off with their businesses. I started Calls That Count in the early days working from home, and to get things going it's often the best option. Working from home is comparatively low cost, and you're not having to commit yourself to potentially expensive outgoings before you've started to bring some money in. In an ideal world you would have a dedicated office at home, a room which is yours and yours alone for the purposes of being where you work, it doesn't double up for any other secondary use like a bedroom, kitchen, living room or bathroom! That said, for many of you it won't be possible to dedicate a room just for your business, and that's fine too just as long as you have a corner somewhere, or a table top big enough to place your computer, a few files and oh yes your telephone! When I started Calls That Count my mission control was actually in the corner of a bedroom, so I ran my whole business from about 4 square feet of space. Doesn't matter, remember that well known saying "perception is reality" The people you'll be calling to talk about your product/service are not going to make a decision on whether to do business with you based on how flash your office is, they'll be making decisions based on much more important things than that, like how you come across on the telephone, are you confident, do they get on with you, do you make sense, do you add up, do you talk intelligently, are you listening, those kinds of things. So step one then is to decide where in the house you are going to be working from and importantly dialing out from. It's important wherever that space is in the house that you view it in exactly the same way that you would if you were working in an office somewhere. You need to treat that space even if it is only 4 square feet like a professional working environment. If you don't, believe me people will know it when they are speaking with you on the phone. I've spoken a lot about this over the years, the fact that people can actually "feel" and "see" you down a telephone line. Call me old fashioned but I think if you're working from home there's a lot to be said for getting up, getting dressed into your business clothes and leaving the house. Go somewhere business like for a coffee like a hotel foyer where you can plan your day and then "arrive at work" I used to do this and initially got some funny looks from the neighbours seeing me leave for work and then return an hour later. Lazy so and so I bet they thought! So, what do we need kit wise to get our calling started. We'll the beauty of telemarketing is that it's really easy to assemble what you need, a well known online marketplace platform will have plenty of choice for you.

- **DESK/CHAIR:** Your desk/chair combination needs to be really comfortable. You won't be in the right place mentally if all you can think of is how painful your back is, your neck is, your legs are. Height/back adjustable chair is a must to make sure that you maximise ergonomics in your favour. In a nutshell you want to be able to work in comfort at all times, just common sense.

- **COMPUTER:** A decent PC- I am not a tech expert so all I'm going to say here is that you need a good PC with enough oomph (technical term) to make sure your spread sheets are not freezing on you and your cursor is not 10 seconds behind your keyboard strokes. (we've all been there). You want one that is pretty much a blank canvass rather than one you've commandeered from elsewhere in the house. Your kids won't be too happy if you've nicked the one they use for gaming, and neither will you be when they nick it back and destroy all your calling data. Naturally you'll need to make sure your PC has the applications you'll need to successfully carry out your prospecting activity, so Excel, Word, Outlook etc.

- **PHONE:** A business telephone- again I'm not here to go into the various merits of one make over another but like a trowel is the tool of choice for a bricklayer, the phone is your tool of the trade. You won't see a good brickie skimping on his trowel and neither should you with your phone. Again, it's business. I know it sounds a bit weird, but believe me when you pick up that receiver you need to know its business, you want your phone to be a business phone that feels good in your hand, has all the various bits and pieces that you'd expect on a business phone, like being digital, caller ID, speaker phone, number memory. So, not for example one shaped like a banana that someone bought you for a laugh one Christmas. It's business, get a business phone. You will also want to consider a headset for both comfort and to prevent any repetitive strain injury. Without a headset over time you can cause yourself quite a bit of neck strain as your head will be tilted at an angle over an extended period of time. That said, I've spoken with plenty of sales people that just can't get on with them, I'm one of them, and I can't put my finger on it but it just doesn't "feel" the same when I'm talking with someone wearing a headset. Health and Safety says wear one, you decide for yourself. If you're running your business from home you really do need to have a dedicated phone line. I'd also definitely advocate investing in an outsourced call handling service so that when you're on the phone/not available/out you can rest assured that your calls are being handled professionally. Very few people leave messages on answer phones but they will leave one for you with a real live person who's explaining why you are unavailable right now. Having your calls answered gives your business a much more professional image too.

- **LINED PADS:** Good supply of A4 lined pads and pens that work. Note taking as we'll see later in the book is very, very important when making outbound calls, so never be without the trusted A4 pad. Important by the way that it's A4 and not A5, you'll see why later on.

- **STOPWATCH:** A stopwatch – doesn't matter if this is a mechanical/electrical one that actually sits on your desk, or a virtual one that you can have on your desk top. The main point is that you have one and you can easily turn it on and off. (I'll be covering why you need a stopwatch in a while but for now just be aware that you're going to need one) Plenty of options for downloads of free stopwatch apps from the web, and again a bit of online shopping will easily pick up an inexpensive stopwatch if you want the real deal.

- **METHOD TO RECORD YOUR CALLS:** You will find it incredibly useful to be able to record some of your calls to listen to how you come across, and how you are engaging with the people you're speaking with. Take it from me, not many people actually like the way they sound, but that's not the point of it, it's purely to hear how what you're saying and how you're saying it is being received by the other person.

Get in the habit of randomly recording some calls each day and listen to them back. Over time you'll gain a huge amount of confidence from hearing just how far your skills have developed. In particular keep on your desktop recordings of really great calls that you've made where everything just clicked. These can serve as a regular confidence builder and are well worth listening to before you start a calling session.

There are some excellent systems which enable you to dial into a number first before you make your call, enter a code and that then activates the call recording. You can then retrieve your call from an online system where your recordings are held "in the cloud" for you to listen to/download.

I don't want to get into too deeply the legislation around call recording but suffice to say that if you're recording purely for your own quality control/educational purposes it is absolutely fine.

The Telecommunications (Lawful Business Practice) (Inter-ception of Communications) Regulations 2000 cover call recording and do state that if you are recording calls of someone else within your business however, then you do need to let them know.

It doesn't though stipulate that the recipient also be informed. The Direct Marketing Association Code of Practice does consider it Best Practice but it is recognised that clearly this is not always possible or practical especially in a sales call environment.

As with all matters marketing for further advice/guidance talk with The Direct Marketing Association.

If you are working from an office environment the tools of the trade remain the same and just as for the person working at home needs to have a dedicated space for the calling activity, the same goes for the office. At both home and in the office environments there are many distractions, but one could argue that more so when you are working with other people. One thing I can tell you is that whatever your situation is, to get the most from working the phone you need to have a dedicated focus on what you are doing. Therefore, if in an office, particularly open plan you might want to consider three "buffer partitions" to go around your desk. It's amazing how just sectioning off your workspace a little bit can help you to get focused on what you are doing. So if you are reading this book because your Company have asked you to start making outbound calls talk to them about helping you to create your own workspace that will conducive to you being able to concentrate fully on what you are doing. If you have your own individual office either as a business owner or as an employee then effectively your dedicated calling space is ready made.

Your environment is everything when making calls, so don't skip on making yourself completely comfortable where you'll be working.

Ok, so we have decided where we are working, now we need to look at the when.

When to make your calls

You will hear all sorts of stories from people about when is and isn't the best time to make business sales and marketing calls. These conversations are usually started by people who don't like making sales calls and are trying to justify that by putting off people who do want to crack on with it. Their reasoning usually goes something like this: "You shouldn't call people on a Monday because on Mondays they have just got back into work after the weekend and the last thing they want to get is a sales call. Tuesdays and Wednesday's aren't great because it's the middle of the week and they will be up to their eyes in it. Thursdays are a poor day to call people because they are trying to rush through unfinished tasks as they only have one more day before the weekends, and that's

Friday. Now Fridays are not good to call people because they are thinking about the weekend. You should therefore leave your call until Monday, but hold on before you do because Mondays are not a good time to call people because...

I've heard them all over the years. Don't call people before usual office hours as they'll see it as an intrusion. Don't call them during usual office hours because they are working. Don't call at lunch time they'll be at lunch. Whatever you do, don't call after normal working hours they will be really annoyed with you, especially after a busy day.

Have you noticed a pattern here? Bottom line is that if someone is determined not to make sales calls because they don't want to make them there will always be a good reason they will find not to. This all comes back to the mindset we spoke about earlier in the book. Get the mindset right and everything else will click into place.

Now let me tell you based on many years experience when the absolute optimum time is to call someone. Are you ready? Ok, here it is. The answer is anytime. Anytime is a good time to call. Let me say that again ANYTIME is a good time to call. You can reach people early in the morning, during the day, lunchtime, afternoon, and evening. I've set sales appointments with people at 6.30am in the morning before the normal working day starts, and I've set them at 8.00pm in the evening when everyone else apart from me and the person I'm calling have gone home. I've set them when I've been told the only time I'll get to speak with someone is on a Saturday morning because that's when they go into the office to catch up on their admin.

The early morning and after office hours evening time slots are particularly interesting. I've come to realise over my career that many senior people within businesses, companies and organisations get in early and stay late. They get at their desk by 6.00am, 6.30am or 7.00am to get a head start on the day, and also are often still at their desks at 7.00pm and 8.00pm at night (By the way just as an aside, I thoroughly recommend and early start to you. Whole separate topic but suffice to say, start early, get going, plan your day, you'll feel great when you do. If you're someone who feels there are not enough hours in the day you can find two or three extra ones easily by starting earlier.) Thing is that not many other people get in at that time, or stay as late. For example the reception team won't be there so therefore your call is much more likely to be picked up direct by "whoever" is in (and we know who that is likely to be). Far from being seen as an intrusion as some people would have you think my experience is that quite the opposite is true. People who make decisions, get things done, get in early, and go home late are the sort of people who will admire and be appreciative of your initiative and work ethic. More often than not they will be happy to have a conversation (there's that word again) with you because you're calling in the "quiet before the storm" period, or the peace and quiet after the days mayhem. In fact I've had many an early morning call with someone which has started off by us having a bit of banter about them not being the only people who get in early. There's also something else that happens when two people are having a conversation at a time of day that wouldn't normally be considered to be usual working hours. People are much happier to just be themselves, and let a lot of the "business persona" nonsense go. I liken it to a similar feeling people have when they've been asked to go into work at a weekend in the own clothes. Yes they are at work, but their demeanour is much more relaxed and they are being much more like the real them. People feel like they don't have to put on any kind of alter ego because other people often aren't around. By the way isn't it funny when you see people out of their usual working clothes and in casual gear, often they just look and come across completely differently. That's because in my opinion most people at work are playing a role, they are not being themselves. Your mission as you'll see is to be yourself at ALL times, and never to be drawn into the game of charades that often takes place in the buyer/seller relationship.

Here's another way of looking at why your call is more likely to reach a decision maker if you get creative with when you're calling. Imagine your call is like a plane trying to land at Heathrow Airport during peak hours. There are so many other planes trying to land that often pilots are asked to fly a holding pattern by the air traffic control. We've all been there, left, straight, left, straight, left, left straight, and then all of a sudden you go down pretty quickly and land. Or sometimes, you're up there in the holding pattern for what seems like ages and then actually you don't get to land at all, you're sent somewhere else entirely due to bad weather, or other operational issues. However, I can never remember being on a flight scheduled to land in a quiet time slot when there isn't much air traffic around, being placed in a holding pattern, there's no need, the pilot can just go straight in. In the world of business to business telemarketing then, you're the pilot, the planes are your calls, and air traffic controllers in the tower are people on reception to potentially delay your call. I say potentially because as we'll see later on the matter of whether or not you're your call will be put through owes as much to the game of chance as it does to the game of skill. Holding patterns for you will be things like being told someone is in a meeting when they're not, being asked to send an e mail, or write to someone, being told they're out when they're not, or call later etc. So it's well worth a try to schedule you flights during quieter times of the day/evening. That's not to say of course that you shouldn't call at other times too. As I said, anytime is a good time to call. It's just that if we're going to be "flying" during the peak periods we need to make sure we are familiar with all the controls! By the way let me say straight away that receptionists are absolutely not people whose mission it is to make your life difficult. They are actually as you'll soon discover potentially your biggest help, it's just that when the skies are busy it's their job to put the holding patterns in place that's all, and if they didn't, the people for whom they take calls just wouldn't be able to cope with the volume.

How many calls should you make each day?

Without over simplifying things the answer here is as many as you can. Again it depends on what your personal situation is. For example if you are a sole trader business owner then making outbound calls is going to form just one aspect of what you have to do to keep the show on the road. However, if you're someone working within a business and you're reading this book because you've recently been asked to take on the role of making outbound calls then it's likely that a larger percentage of your time will be spent on the phone. The rule of thumb though whatever your situation is that regular consistent daily prospecting will always outperform the boom or bust mentality. There is little point in hitting the phone like a madman for a week making hundreds and hundreds of calls if after that week it all falls by the wayside.

An hour a day keeps the sales on their way

You can achieve some phenomenal results by dedicating just an hour, one single hour a day, about 20 calls, every day to people to see if you can help them. One of the things that people tell me that puts them off making outbound calls is that they have this perception that they have to have the phone glued to their ear for hours and hours on end. Well, take it from me you don't. An hour a day of quality uninterrupted outbound calling can transform your sales revenues. Put a sign on your home office door when you're calling that says "Do not disturb, sales funnel filling in progress" and tell everyone who may be in at the time that it's really important that every day during your dedicated calling time that you are left to be completely focused on what you are doing. If you're in an office, let your co workers know that unless something is absolutely a must do now urgent action that if left could have serious consequences, you are unavailable and are not to be disturbed. Over time your hour a day will build and build in momentum and you can have the peace of mind that you're adding to your funnel of short medium and longer term opportunities every single day. Think about it like this too. If your sales cycle is three months from the time you first speak with someone to the time you actually end up agreeing to do business together then it's just common sense that for every day you miss making your calls you are delaying the date on which you'll be able to monetise your activity. So every day without prospecting is delaying the day when your best opportunities come out the end of your sales funnel. Make the calls every day, fill the funnel consistently, and then inevitably a number of these opportunities will come out of the other end. The mistake many make however is to add to the funnel in fits and starts. "I'll make some calls tomorrow" The problem here of course is that kind of activity leads to the sales funnel being full in places but completely empty in others. The end result is that the boom or bust, feast or famine scenario occurs.

Regular consistent prospecting every day will pay you back a thousand times over. Don't kid yourself you can make the calls up another day, it doesn't work like that.

Block off religiously the hour a day you are going to make your calls and protect that time as if it were a meeting with your most important client. Don't let anyone or anything come between you and your daily commitment to get on the phone. You will thank me for repeating this and hammering the point home. Believe me I know exactly what it's like to be building a business where there are a seemingly never ending list of demands on your time. Have I always managed to stick to my hour a day?, no of course not, we're all human, but what I can tell you is that during those times I didn't, I subsequently felt the negative effects of not prospecting consistently, and so will you if you don't take the hour a day mentality seriously. It was never any surprise to me either that as soon as normal service was resumed my business immediately felt the positive effects of regular consistent sales funnel filling.

How much money can you generate from your prospecting?

What if I said to you that one cold call or a follow up call could generate £150,000? Or another one could make £50,000, or yet another £40,000? Or that many others could generate contracts in the multi multi thousands bracket? Would that make you want to get on the phone? Of course it would, you'd be mad not to right? Think about the lifetime value of winning a client. It isn't just the business you win initially from your cold call to set an appointment from which you win the deal, but it's all of the lifetime follow on business too. Seen in those terms, it's easy for a single cold call to be worth literally thousands and thousands in sales revenue to your business. In order to find the contracts worth this kind of money you are going to have to be prepared to dedicate yourself to an hour a day. Can you do that?

For those of you who think the above examples are out of your reach then think again. All of them are real life examples of cold calls I've made either for clients or for my own business.

You may be thinking that well ok Robbie that's alright for you doing that you probably came into this world holding a phone, but there's no way I could make calls that result in that kind of revenue. Wrong. You can, and you will. Do the activity consistently and the results will come, but it all starts with taking action.

Let me give you a brief overview of some example of cold calls that have led to big business. You'll see that the industry sectors involved are all quite varied so these kinds of contracts are up for grabs by anybody who is willing to drop their perceptions of what they think cold calling, prospecting whatever you want to call it is all about, relax with the process and just call people!

In the interests of confidentiality I've omitted Company and individual names but all examples are real life calls made by me, or members of my team.

You'll see with some of these examples that a cold call has been used in conjunction with a second form of communication to initiate the sales process. Often you'll need to use different communication methods to move prospects along your sales funnel but it all starts with a cold call or sometimes it starts with another activity and is then moved along with a follow up call.

Ten phone call examples from the real world

Example one "Who told you to call me today?"

To help you fully understand the massively positive implications that came about as a result of this particular cold call, I first need to give you some background. When I first started Calls That Count in 2007, it won't surprise you to know that a very large percentage of the initial business that I won came about as a result of me picking up my phone and calling people to introduce my appointment setting and lead generation services. (That's still how we win most of our business today too) On one of my first prospecting sessions I made contact with a Company in the construction business. Their main specialism was in the refurbishment of commercial office spaces, sometimes referred to as "office fit out". I spoke with one of the Directors and it turned out that yes, they had been recently talking about different ways they could generate more appointments with companies in the planning process for refurbishment of their office spaces. I set an appointment for me to go in and find out more about their situation. It turned out that although the Company was clearly excellent at what they did and they were able to show me a catalogue of very impressive fit outs they had completed, it was clear that from a sales perspective, getting out there and "selling" what they had to offer they found a struggle. One of the Directors who had been given the role of selling the Company openly admitted to me that he found sales difficult. He was superb from a practical perspective and a real expert at what they did but picking the phone up to get the ball rolling was definitely a hurdle for him. I talked through with them what type of companies would be an ideal target market for them and the end result of the meeting was that I was going to deliver a 10 day initial pilot telemarketing campaign with the objective of setting up appointments. So, I went back to my office, pulled together a great data list, did my homework on the Company and the industry that they operated in and then scheduled my first week of calls. So, there's the background, and here's what happened next.

First few days as I expected resulted in uncovering some really valuable leads with Facilities Managers at different sites telling me about projects which were scheduled to take place, but a long way off. However, they were still good leads to drop into my client's pipeline. Then I made a call into a Company that went like this. Call one resulted in me being told that they had had a change of Facilities Manager and being given a new contact name. I asked if he was available and I was told, no he wouldn't be around until later that day. I asked for a direct dial to reach him on which I was given. Call two later that day went like this "Hello John, My name's Robbie, I'm with ABC Company, we work with Facilities Managers at Blue Chip organizations nationally helping them to deliver refurbishment projects on time and on budget. I've been directed to you as I understand that you're now overseeing Facilities for the Company, is that right?" "Yes, It's interesting that you should call, tell me a bit more about what you do" My contacts reaction demonstrates just how much the phrase "You've got to be in it to win it" is so true. I outlined some of the types of projects my client had completed and he then said "Who asked you to call me today?" I just explained that they were exactly the kind of Company we'd helped in the past and that was the reason for my contact, and that it wasn't specifically because someone had asked me to call him. He said "Actually Robbie, we have a project that needs completing here, and we're under a bit of time pressure with it. We've spoken with a few people but haven't made a decision yet" He then happily told me more about the project, what was involved, and what he was looking for. I set an appointment for my client to go in and meet him, and the end result of my "cold call" was my client winning a £150,000 fit out contract. The job was completed, my client as you can imagine was delighted, and the Facilities Manager was equally happy as he had dealt quickly and successfully with something that was clearly a pressing issue for him.

No magic in what happened here. I just made a call, had a bit of good fortune and uncovered an absolutely superb sales opportunity. I just had a conversation. If you have enough conversations in the right way great things will happen. These types of sales opportunities are out there waiting for your business too.

We continued to work with this client for a number of years, so not a bad return for picking the phone up and dialing a number.

Example two "I doubt it's worth your while coming in to see us"

I made a cold call into a Company that provides catering equipment with associated maintenance, repair and support services. They are a long established and well respected Company in their industry. My contact list had identified the Sales Director for me. I got through and we got on well straight away. He was a lovely guy, with a huge amount of experience in sales generally but specifically within their industry. We had a chat about how they currently generate sales appointments and leads and what came to light was that the sales team didn't have enough time to be making as many outbound prospecting calls as they'd like to. Due to the success of the business, their time was often taken up with account management visits looking after their existing client base. This meant that their pipeline building for new clients sometimes had to take a back seat. I suggested that I went in to talk with them and my contact said to me "I doubt it's worth your while coming to see us, as it's unlikely you'll sell us anything"

I knew from the way our conversation had gone that there was definitely scope for us to work together and his response was what is sometimes referred to as a "smokescreen objection" He was just throwing it out there to see how I'd react. A poor response would have been "Well, if you don't think that you'd go for what we offer, then maybe we should talk again in six months when things have changed" This kind of response simply would have highlighted an attitude of "I only want to see you if there's something in it for me" which is a very poor attitude to have in sales, and prospects will see you coming a mile away. My actual response was "That's ok. I'd like to come and see you just to learn more about your situation, and yes of course I'll outline how I feel I may be able to help. However, you'll be the judge as to whether we work together or not, not me, and if at the end of the meeting it's decided that we don't, then no problem, it's always good to meet people and make contacts regardless of the outcome"

I set the appointment, and we ended up working with this client consistently for over five years. Additionally we were recommended by them to other clients. All of that business too, can be attributed to my original cold call.

Example three "I got your voicemail"

Don't underestimate the power of leaving a well thought out powerful voicemail message. Here's an example of where a cold call led to me leaving a message that in turn led to a new client. I called a Company in the ventilation sector. After 3 attempts to reach the Sales Director I decided to leave a voicemail. It was a Friday afternoon at 4.30pm. The message I left was. "Hi John, my name's Robbie from Calls That Count, we help Sales Directors at Companies to increase sales revenues by setting quality, qualified sales appointments. I've missed you a few times so just wanted to say that if over the weekend you are thinking at all about ways to win more new clients then I'd welcome an opportunity to talk to you. If not, no problem, hope you have a good weekend. My number is 01206 832 280, once again that's Robbie at Calls That Count about winning more new business."

Monday morning I came into the office. I already had a message from my reception team waiting for me. John had left his own message. "John from ABC called, said he picked up your voicemail and wants to know more. Please call him"

I called John back (now obviously a warm call) and we had a really good conversation about his current situation. We arranged to meet, and shortly after that we started work with them setting appointments for John to attend, and building a nice pipeline of leads too.

This is a good example of different tools working together, the initial cold call and then the voicemail message, and finally the follow up call.

Example four "Are you psychic?"

I received a call in the office one day from the sales manager of a Company we were working with in the drinks industry. He told me that he'd just driven past a huge site at the side of the motorway and all he had was the Company name but he thought it looked like the kind of Company they should be working with. He asked if I could see what I could do in terms of finding out who the best contact was at the Company and to see if I could get the ball rolling. A bit of desk research on the internet took me to the Company's website and from there a quick look at the "Our People" section pointed me in the right direction. I checked the telephone number against the CTPS to make sure it was clear and made my call. It was one of those multi option switchboards and unfortunately my contact was not one of the options so I used a strategy I call "sideways in" to get put through to the right department. Basically I selected an option from the menu which I knew was not the office I wanted but equally I knew I'd get to speak with a human being! From memory, I think it was accounts I went through to. When I got through, I apologised for having "misrouted" myself on their switchboard and then told them who it was that I had been trying to reach. As often happens using this approach I was transferred internally straight to the direct line of my contact. When she answered the phone, I simply asked her for some help. I explained exactly what had happened, namely that we had seen her Company's site from the motorway and were keen to introduce ourselves and see whether what we had to offer was something she was happy to talk about, or was something that from her point of view she was looking to review. Her answer was quite simply "Are you psychic!" "I'm not sure how you managed to get straight through to me as I don't normally take sales calls without having first seen something first but actually yes, you've called at a very good time. I've had a contract on my desk from our current supplier that should have been signed a week ago, and I haven't signed it." I said "If you don't mind me saying so, that sounds like there is something about your current deal that maybe you're not quite happy with?" She said "Well that's a pretty accurate assessment!" I asked her more about her current situation and then simply said "Would you mind if I made a suggestion? Based on what you've told me it seems to make sense for us to get together and discuss those areas that are causing you concern. Shall we do that?" She agreed the appointment for the very next day with my client, and they won a very lucrative long term deal which is still in place to this day.

I hope that you're starting to see a pattern here with these examples. It's just common sense. No magical secret sales techniques, just common sense, persistence and a desire to call people and have a conversation about where they are now and whether what we have to offer can help. That's it plain and simple.

This next one is a great example of how a call about one thing can lead to another.......

Example five "Do you do training?"

I made a call for Calls That Count into a Company operating in the education sector. With some help from the receptionist (that's right some help, receptionists contrary to popular belief amongst many traditional sales training systems, can actually be your best allies in helping you move your sale along) I ended up with the mobile number of the Regional Sales Director. When I called he was about to go into a meeting but in the short time we'd spoken together I'd said enough just to tweak his interest level. He asked me to call him back next day when he'd be in the office. I called at the agreed time and after a decent conversation (there's that word again) about how they currently develop new sales opportunities it became clear that he already had someone in the office who was tasked with making outbound calls. He then said "Do you do training?" It turned out that his internal sales person was facing a few challenges with certain aspects of the sales process. End result here was that I went in and delivered a one day bespoke telephone marketing course for his sales person.

So, a cold call about one service (sales appointment setting) resulted in me winning some business for another service (sales training)

Always be ready to be flexible on your calls. Conversations can take different directions, keep your ears open and you may well uncover opportunities for other products or services that you can help with apart from the one you called about.

Example six "What do you mean?"

I read an article about an industrial equipment distributor that gave me the name of the Sales Manager. I called the Company but he wasn't available but I managed to obtain his e mail address. Instead of "What's John's e mail address please" I used, "If I wanted to reach John by e mail, what address would I send to for him please?" It's a subtle difference and there is some psychology at play within the words but basically it's less direct, less intrusive and doesn't feel like you're putting the person you're speaking with on the spot. Try it, and you'll find the amount of times you're able to obtain people's direct e mail addresses increases. Anyway, I sent the e mail below:

"Hello John, I called earlier but missed you. My name's Robbie Stepney and I'm with Calls That Count, we help Sales Managers at Companies to increase sales revenues by setting quality, qualified sales appointments. Just making contact to ask if you are looking at ways to win more new business. I'd welcome an opportunity to talk with you. Warmest Regards, Robbie"

I received the following reply within an hour:

"What do you mean?" In other words the tone of my e mail was such that it tweaked my prospects interest, he wanted to know more, and that is the start of a conversation which is what we're always looking for.

From here I arranged via e mail a convenient time to give him a further call to discuss further. The result of that (you've guessed it...) conversation was that I set up an appointment for me to go in and meet with him. We won a new contract and delivered a successful campaign with more to follow.

Interesting thing here is that in this case it was combination of cold call, e mail, and then a follow up call that won the day.

Some people will tell you never to use e mail before you have spoken with someone first, In a word nonsense! In today's business development world you need to be knitting different tools together to help you win sales. It all starts with a call, but from there use as many other tools as you can to build the relationship, e mail, hard copy letter, voicemail whatever it takes to achieve your objective of speaking with and then meeting with your prospect.

Another way to do it is to reverse the sequence, mix it up a bit, so send an e mail or letter first then follow up by phone.

After all, people respond to different things. Some people may take your call first time, others may not, but they may respond to a well thought out voicemail message, or a carefully worded respectful e mail. The key is activity, activity, activity. Doing as many things as you can to move you further along the sales process.

Example seven "Might be something we'd look at"

One of my colleagues called into a commercial cleaning Company and spoke with the Sales Director. It turned out that the Company had been talking about ways to increase sales activity as they were due to be moving into new larger premises. She said "It might be something we'd look at" "He set an appointment for me to go and meet with the Sales Director and her General Manager. This initial appointment was cancelled due to some extremely poor weather and we rescheduled. As the re scheduled appointment was some way off, nearer the time I called to check that everything was still ok. It turned out that that the upcoming move had proved to be more challenging than they'd first thought and so appointment number two was also cancelled. I agreed that we'd make contact again in a few months once things had settled down a bit. We called back three months later and set appointment number three which I duly attended. We won a new contract and the interesting thing here is that our clients had appreciated our understanding and patience when we had to re schedule things on two occasions. There's a lesson here. Working the phone is about building short, medium and longer term opportunities. You can't expect everything to just happen within a short timescale. You've got to understand that things happen within peoples businesses which mean the sales process may stall for a while. It doesn't mean that they don't want to do business with you. Be patient, call back when you say you will and be guided by your prospect as to when they are ready to move forward. Don't push it, prod it, force it, let is just happen. Of course you need to be sure that your prospect is being "real" with you about any reasons for not being able to stick to the game plan, but if you've been having the kind of conversations with them that I've been advocating in this book then you will be.

So to recap, this example is about a cold call uncovering an opportunity, followed by persistent but patient follow up leading to a sale.

Example eight – "Give me a call"

A lot of you will be going networking every week which is great, but here's a question. Are you also great at making calls to those people you've met to cement the relationship? Many of you will feel as anxious about making phone calls to people you've met at a networking event, or other business seminar as you do making cold calls. Your mind will be playing the same kind of tricks on you. So, here's an example of how a single call following a brief conversation at a networking event lead to a six year contract for ongoing appointment setting services for my Company, and hopefully will help you to see that it really is worth picking your phone and talking with people you've met.

I was asked to go to a networking event one Friday evening. I was sat at a table and was introduced to a guy who was the Business Development Manager for a Company in the creative sector. We got chatting and it turned out that he had been looking at ways to increase the number of sales appointments he was attending. He was actually someone who was very comfortable in making calls himself, and I would imagine very good at it too, but he just didn't have enough hours in the day to make the calls, attend his meetings as well as dealing with his other commitments. I briefly explained that the time factor was one of the main reasons Companies used Calls That Count. At that point, we were interrupted by a presentation that was about to take place and he just said to me "Good to meet you Robbie, give me a call" We managed to quickly exchange cards and that was last I saw of him that night as the event wrapped up pretty shortly afterwards.

Now, that kind of encounter is happening thousands of times every single day at business events up and down the country. I wonder how many of those "Give me a call" comments are actually acted upon.

Well, here's what I did. I called the guy, we had a conversation about his situation, arranged to meet at his offices and that was the start of a six year contract.

Again two forms of activity working together. A networking encounter followed up with a phone call. No magic, no difficult techniques involved, but there's one thing for sure. If I hadn't of made the call nothing would have happened, nothing. It's action that makes things happen.

Example Nine- "That made a lot of sense to me"

As well as running my own telephone marketing and sales 1-1 coaching and training courses, I'm now also regularly invited along as a speaker at various types of event to talk to business people about overcoming their fear of the phone and using it as a powerful addition to their sales and marketing plans. Just as an aside, becoming a speaker is a great way to be seen as the expert in your chosen field and I can tell you that every single time you get on your feet to talk there will always be people in that audience who really connect with what you have to say and will want to work with you in one way or another. I'd strongly recommend to you that if you are not speaking at events at the moment to start to develop your speaking skills and to put yourself forward as someone event organisers can call upon when they want your particular topic covered. There is a massive range of networking groups out there and often these groups are looking for speakers. You'll need to push your comfort zone though (which is a great thing to do) as public speaking is right up there with cold calling amongst business people as an activity they'd rather not do, you may feel that way about it too, so if you can push yourself to do it you'll be gaining a big advantage over those who can't or more specifically won't do it.

I was invited to speak at an event one weekend where the audience were there to learn about different ways to boost sales in their business. Al sorts of topics were covered from websites, to SEO, to online lead capture, networking, referrals etc.

In my talk I just explained that it's great to have as many different types of lead generation activity taking place within a business as possible but the bottom line was that at some stage in the sales process someone is going to have to pick the phone up and call the contact to progress things. I said that you can have all the leads you like, but unless your business is one where the complete transaction from start to finish is conducted electronically without the need for personal interaction, somewhere along the line there needs to be a conversation. I also covered a bit on how to structure a call but the thrust of my short talk was really about just getting people to see that there is a place for the telephone in every business or Company and to leave it out is to be missing a trick.

On the Monday following the event I received and e mail from a guy who had his own technology Company. In his message he said "I enjoyed your talk on Saturday and that made a lot of sense to me, can we talk?"

It won't surprise you to know that I called him there and then, we set up a good time to talk in more detail and we started working together.

Again, one form of business development (speaking) working with a telephone follow up.

Example 10 – "Can you send me some prices on your services?"- a web enquiry

In your business you are likely to be receiving a range of incoming enquiries via your website. Often these enquiries are asking for information on what you charge for your services. The danger here is that without the personal phone conversation to dig a little deeper into what their situation is you can end up just replying to these requests with an e mail giving them some figures and you never hear from them again.

At Calls That Count we receive incoming enquiries all the time too. We will never under any circumstances reply in full to an enquiry without first having a conversation with the enquirer. You can learn so much more about them that way, and so when you do cover the issue of price you know that it is a proposal specific to their requirements, and from their point of view they have had an opportunity to hear the value of what you offer, not just the price which on its own is a meaningless figure. If your enquirer has not given a telephone number, then do some research and find one. If you can't find one then e mail them back thanking them for their enquiry and just explaining that in order to give them the information they need specific to their situation you'd like to suggest a brief phone conversation first and can they give you the best number to reach them on. After all, if they won't give you a number you've got to question the strength of their enquiry in the first place.

Recently I received an e mail from a Sales Director of a very large overseas equipment manufacturer. The e mail stated that they were looking for telemarketing representation in the UK and he added "can you send me some information on what you can offer with prices"

I called the contact and the first thing he commented on was that I had been one of only three people who had telephoned him to talk further/find out more out of the seven Companies he had contacted. On the basis we are talking about telemarketing Companies here I found this to be quite unbelievable! The others had responded, quite generically with an overview of what they could do with prices.

Anyway, we had a long conversation that enabled me to subsequently put together a proposal based on his actual situation and objectives. I received a reply to say that we had been shortlisted in the top two suppliers and I'd get my decision at the end of that week.

The end result was that on this occasion we didn't win the business, because another Company had included what I felt were some quite unrealistic promises in terms of what would be delivered within a set time frame. I wasn't prepared to mirror that as a means to win the work.

That said, the Sales Director called me and thanked me for the professional way I had dealt with his enquiry, my subsequent proposal, and as he put it "Also Robbie, the hugely professional way that you dealt with the news that your Company had not been successful on this occasion, but rest assured we will be back in touch with you should the promises made fail to materialise"

I've ended with this example of the benefits of a good follow up call to demonstrate that no, you don't always win, but if you make the calls and show people you are genuinely interested in helping them the door will always be left open for you.

Another point worth noting from this example is also that you should never feel pressured to match another offer even if you think it unrealistic just to win the work. Stick to the principles of being completely truthful, honest, up front and operate with the highest level of integrity at all times in every dealing you have with customers and potential customers and you'll be the winner. Winning business by over promising is a poor short term strategy that will come back to haunt you. Do not do it.

The ten examples I've given above in terms of invoiced value were worth a combined figure of approximately £385,000. Does it pay to pick your phone up?

Chapter 5

How to get through to the right person

Over the years I've heard all sorts of views on how best to "get past the Gatekeeper" to reach your decision maker. I'll come back to the word "Gatekeeper" in a second but for now let me put you at ease by telling you about the rule of three, or to be more specific the rule of thirds. The rule of thirds is something that I've come to realise over the years and it should make you feel considerably more confident when making your calls. You'll be more confident because it takes away all of the uncertainty of what kind of reaction you may encounter when you get through to the switchboard or reception of your target Company. Knowledge as they say is power. What the rule of thirds dictates is that regardless of what you say or how you say it, as long as you're polite and professional, there is a third of all Companies that you call where you are going to get put through to your contact. You will call, ask to speak with John Jones and a few seconds later you'll be talking to John Jones. It's that simple. The person on reception or whoever picks the phone up will be only too pleased to put you through. These types of Companies operate a refreshing open door policy where if you call and you have the name of the person you want to speak with they'll do their level best to put you through. They'll also help you with things like giving you your contacts direct line number if they are unavailable, their e mail, and will also be really helpful by giving you the very best time to call back for them. Sounds great, right?

It's not all plain sailing though because the rule of thirds also dictates that regardless of what you say or how you say you are not going to be put through to your contact at a third of all companies you call (there are other ways you can try to reach him or her and we'll look at those later, but if you're going through the front door so to speak you are not going to get to talk with them) You can study cold calling inside out and upside down but for this third it won't matter, you won't be speaking with who you want to speak with. You will be blocked at every turn and generally find these kind of calls are pretty tough going right from the start. You'll sense that as soon as you start speaking with the person who's picked the phone up that they're actually quite hostile to incoming callers and unlike our first third they won't be doing anything to make your life easier or point you in the right direction in any way. Take my advice here, if you ever call a Company and you feel that however professional polite and reasonable you are being that the person you're speaking with is quite adamant that they don't want to put you through or help you in any way, thank them politely for their time and just get off the phone. We all know the saying "You can win the battle but lose the war" In this kind of situation often sales people become defensive about why they can't be put through and go into some kind of battle of wits with the person on the phone. They may feel a bit better for doing so but they're still not going to get through and are in my opinion just burning energy which could be better applied to another call.

So, we've looked at the first two thirds, those where you'll always get through, and those where you never will! (when calling the Company's main number) So for the mathematicians amongst you that leaves the final third or as I like to call it the third that's up for grabs. This is the third of Companies where there is no set policy either in favour of putting callers through or not, and the decision as to whether to put you through or help you will be dictated by the way you come across, the words you use, and the demeanour you convey down the telephone. In other words the first impression you have created in the mind of the person you are speaking with. Make no mistake about it everyone you speak with over the telephone will be making mental pictures in their mind as to what kind of person you are. These impressions are made very quickly, actually within 5 seconds (no pressure there then!) Now clearly if we can get this right and create the right impression we can edge the odds very much in our favour of getting through to our decision maker contact. The more conversations you have the greater your chance of uncovering sales opportunities. So, that's why it's very worthwhile to explore in detail different ways to win over the up for grabs third. I'm going to take you through step by step how to deal with your initial conversations with people on reception at your target Companies.

Remember don't waste your time or energy trying to win over people at the third of companies where it's a nonstarter. Think about it this way. There are literally thousands and thousands of potential customers for you to speak with. We already know that at a third of the Companies you call you will be put you through, and there's another third where you have a very good chance of getting through, so why worry about the other third? You can't (and won't) win them all, so relax and have fun with it, let them go.

With practice you'll get really good at quickly identifying the "third" you're dealing with. OK, so as I said that should make you feel a bit better knowing that it's absolutely ok on some calls to realise that you're not going to get through and move on. Equally its really great to know as well that there are plenty of people out there who'll be very happy to help you get to speak with your contact, and an equal number who are let's just say "open to persuasion".

From today I want you to stop using the word Gatekeeper. For me, it just conjures up all the wrong mental images of the people who in many cases will be answering your initial calls. Over the years in sales it seems to have become the norm to look upon receptionists and secretaries as people who are there to make sure that your life as a salesperson is as difficult as possible. We have been told that we must "get past the gatekeeper" otherwise we're dead in the water. Well in my opinion this is completely the wrong way to look at this. People who answer the telephone for their business on reception can actually be your best weapon in getting through to who you want to speak with. In my experience many of them contrary to popular belief really do want to help and not hinder you. If you talk to anyone you know who works on a reception for a busy Company and ask them what they think of salespeople they'll more than likely tell you that like everything else in life there are good and there are bad. The good appreciate the job they are doing and are courteous, professional and quite up front in their dealings. They'll also accept the fact that it isn't always possible (or sometimes not possible at all) to speak with who they want to. The bad can be rude, aggressive, suspicious, sarcastic, and never seem to appreciate that often when a receptionist asks you a question it is because dependent on your answer they may in fact re direct you to a far more relevant contact within their Company who is better placed to evaluate your product or service. They are not necessarily asking to be nosey, or to pre judge what you have to offer. My advice is to work with and not against whoever picks up your call. Believe me, be straightforward, courteous, professional, and polite at all times and you'll be surprised at just how much help you'll get from people who have traditionally been cast in the role of "villain". Remember what you read a bit earlier. You know about the three thirds, so don't pre judge and just let your call unfold. There's also another very, very good reason to treat everyone who picks up your call as the most important person in that Company, like they're your final decision maker. That's because sometimes they will be! Over the years I've had plenty of conversations with people who answered my calls and then subsequently turned out to be senior decision makers within the business. So, you never know, treat everyone like VIP's and you won't go far wrong. I've heard plenty of salespeople immediately become quite dismissive of whoever initially answers their call, like they're not important at all, I've never, ever understood that, it's just shooting yourself in the foot before you even start.

First Impressions

Whether you like it or not people will be drawing conclusions about you from the moment they first hear your voice. In fact I'd suggest that you have about 5 seconds on a telephone call to create a great first impression, so make them count. If you get off on the wrong foot it can be very difficult for you to win people back over so this part of the call is very, very important. I want you to think about the last time someone created a really good impression of themselves when they called you about something. What was it about them that you liked? How did they sound? What kind of qualities were they portraying in the tone and speed of their voice, the words they used? Now think about someone who really didn't make a great first impression with you. Why was that? How did they sound? What kind of qualities were they portraying in the tone and speed of their voice, or the words they used? This exercise is useful as it should have highlighted to you how you personally have been affected by first impressions in the past.

The pneumonic below is an easy way to remember why the first impression you create can be the difference between a positive or not so positive outcome on a call.

First

Impressions

Last

Uniqueness of a telephone conversation

Whilst I'm talking to you about first impressions and the best way for you to make your initial telephone approach, you should be aware of something that makes a telephone conversation quite unique. It may seem obvious but over the phone we do not have and neither does the person we're calling the benefit of the visual mode of communication. You cannot see the other person's facial expressions or body language, from which so much can be deduced. This means that you only have the words you use, and to a greater extent the *way* that you say them to get your message across in an effective and persuasive manner. Equally, you will need to decipher how the person you're speaking with is reacting to your call based purely on their words and the *way* that they're saying them. I think too much can be made of body language sometimes, someone scratches their nose and immediately we're led to believe that means they are lying, when actually they might just have an itchy nose! That said, without visual clues you will need to work harder and on in particular your tone of voice to get your sales message to hit the spot.

Don't just take my word for this, there's someone who studied this subject inside out and I'll tell you about him below.

Professor Albert Mehrabian

Professor Albert Mehrabian since the 1960's has pioneered the understanding of communications. He is currently a Professor of Psychology at The University of California in Los Angeles (UCLA). Mehrabian specifically researched and studied the effect of body language and nonverbal communications. The results of his findings are regularly misquoted or oversimplified when explaining how much of what we say is conveyed and understood by the person we're speaking to by different types of communication.

His research can often be seen in various publications presented like this:

7% of the meaning of our message is in the words that we say
38% of the meaning of our message is paralinguistic (the way that we say the words).
55% of the meaning of our message is in our facial expression.

What he *actually* deduced was:

7% of the message **pertaining to feelings and attitudes** is in the words that are spoken.
38% of the message **pertaining to feelings and attitudes** is paralinguistic (the way that the words are said).
55% of **the message pertaining to feelings and attitudes** is in facial expression.

As you can see the difference between the two interpretations is in the words **pertaining to feelings and attitudes.**

When you are on the phone more than anything it is important that the person you are speaking to gets a good feeling about you and equally develops a positive attitude towards you. If they do, then you'll find that your conversation goes a lot more smoothly and is likely to be far more productive. You'll know when this is happening because you just seem to "click" with the person, it all happens really naturally. This can also be described as building "rapport"

You can see from the percentages above just how important *how you say things* is if you want to get your message across.

A couple of clarifications. Mehrabian's model does not apply in the strictest sense to all forms of communication and therefore the percentage values can vary according to the situation.

It does not mean for example that you can only ever get a maximum of 45% of the meaning of your message across using words and the way that you say them on a telephone conversation, as clearly on the phone we are without the visual element completely.

The findings purely signpost for us that we need to work harder in choosing the right words and matching with the right tone to be a successful communicator on the telephone.

Secondly, the model does not extend to very straightforward unequivocal directions. For example, if you were in a building and someone shouted "Fire, fire, get out" you would be able to deduce 100% of the meaning of that message from the words alone. Yes, it would be the case that *how they said it* could dictate just how fast you ran, but essentially you'd get the whole picture from what they said.

So, this section is just here to reinforce the fact that you really only have your words and the way that you say them to paint a picture of what you and your Company is like in the mind of the person you're speaking to.

1st call to a named contact-dialing main Company number

So, now let's take a look at the call plan and language for an initial cold call into a Company where we have the name of our contact.

Before we start though I want to ask you are a question. Are you FIT to call?

F- Are you prepared to give your calling session the **focus** it is going to need if you are to get the best from your conversations. You cannot afford to be easily distracted. Look at it like this, every calling session that is put off, sabotaged halfway through or is delivered in a fragmented way will cost you money in the long run. You are making calls today so that you can reap the benefits in 1 week, 1 month, 3 months, 6 months and over a year down the line. Opportunities you uncover today will pay you back handsomely, so focus, focus, focus.

I – Do you have the **inclination to make these calls?** I can use every means I can to get you to pick your phone up but honestly if you genuinely are not in the mood to talk to people, whatever the reason then wait until you are, just don't leave it too long, as I said above, it will cost you in the long run. We all have off days and we know the difference between feeling genuinely not ourselves, or simply making excuses. You're all grownups, you be the judge on that one.

T- Have you blocked off the **time to make your calls.** However much time you have allocated for this session fiercely protect the time, switch off all other distractions and don't let anything stop you working consistently. The world will not come to an end because you are not available to answer your e mail, or your mobile, so switch them off.

Pre call planning:

- Make sure you have created the right environment to make your calls.

- Open your spreadsheet of contacts.

- Have the website of your first contact's Company up in front of you.

- Take a look at the About Us Section and The News Section and just make a few bullet point notes on their main products and services together with anything that grabs your attention from the news articles

- You'll remember that when looking at the tools of the trade section earlier in the book I said that you'd need a stopwatch. You need a stopwatch so that you can accurately monitor how much actual talk time (time spent actually talking in "live" conversations) you are achieving in your prospecting sessions. Now is the time to get your stopwatch ready so as soon as you connect with your target Company you can start it. As soon as you put your phone down stop the watch. After a while you'll be able to do this really quickly and it will just become second nature, and knowing exactly how much time you're spending in any given week, month, year actually talking to target companies will help you hugely when we look at measuring and improving your statistics in different aspects of the sales process.

- Have your lined pad and a pen to hand, you need to make short bullet point notes throughout your call on anything your contact says that is quite obviously important to them, or is something that you know you'll be able to match to a benefit of what you have to offer at an appropriate point in the conversation.

- Pick up your phone and dial!

Once you're through to reception

Call Opening 1

"Hello, Good afternoon, it's Dave Smith from ABC Company, calling for John Jones please, thank you"

That's it. Straightforward and to the point.

The thinking behind giving your full name and Company upfront is to eliminate the need for questions from the receptionist early on in the process. As I've said there are a thousand different ways to make sales calls but in my opinion some of the more traditional openings can end up making life unnecessarily difficult. Not always, as sometimes however you ask for someone you'll be put through, but it's all about stacking the odds in your favour. For example an alternative approach could be:

"John Jones please"

This though (assuming you're not put through straight away) will often then be met with the response:

"And you are?" or *"Where are you calling from?"* *"Sorry who am I speaking with?"* and numerous variations of the *"Who is this?"* question.

Once someone has felt the need to ask you one question about your call it puts them in the frame of mind to ask another.

Straightforward Approach™ is all about being open, honest, direct, up front, genuine, sincere, candid, forthright easy to deal with polite, and professional at all times. Unfortunately a lot of reception teams are used to salespeople trying to use all sorts of let's say slightly less than transparent methods in order to get through. No one likes to feel like they've had the wool pulled over their eyes and if someone gets the feeling that you're being intentionally evasive of cagey about your call then you can put them in defensive mode straight away. The more honest and straightforward you are the better.

The fact that you are announcing who you are and your Company up front basically says *"look this is who I am, I'm an open book, and I've got nothing to hide here"* Also the language of *"calling for*

John Jones please-thank you" again reinforces the impression that this isn't the first time you've called. You haven't at any point though said that you know John, or another favourite of some sales people *"John knows me"*, or even worse" *I'm returning his call"* or any other variant of these underhand techniques.

They may help to get people past an inquisitive reception team but it all falls apart when John Jones picks his phone up, the receptionist says *"I've got Dave Smith on the phone, says he knows you"* and then 3 seconds into your conversation with John he becomes acutely aware that he does not know you and your credibility and all hope of building a relationship built on trust is destroyed and your call will go downhill rather quickly.

The other subtle piece of psychology in the opening is adding *"please"* immediately followed by *"thank you"*. *"Please"* is simply polite and courteous, and the *"thank you"* which should be said with your voice inflection going down at the end, suggests almost subliminally that you are not expecting to be, and nor is there a reason for you to be challenged in any way, or not put through.

Tone/Pace

When speaking with reception the best tone to have is friendly, professional, human, natural but not over enthusiastic or hyper in any way. This kind of over the top enthusiasm has become synonymous with *"sales call"* and can shoot you in the foot before you've got started. In fact I advocate a very matter of fact approach like you fully expect to be put through with no issues at all (this by the way is how you should be thinking about every call)

Don't fill the space

When you use this opening you'll find that there are 3 things that will happen. The first is that you'll be put straight through. The second is that because the approach is quite different to many calls the receptionist will receive you will almost hear them thinking. They won't put you straight through, but they'll say something like *"One moment please"* and you can tell that they're deciding whether or not to put you through. Whereas normally they may challenge a sales call, here they are unsure because they don't want to be seen to be challenging or questioning someone who based on their tone of voice and language they use clearly fully expects to be put through immediately. After a while, they'll either just put you through or sometimes almost as a way of seeking some kind of confirmation in their own mind that it would be ok to put you through without getting into any kind of hot water they'll come back to you and ask something like *"And can I ask the Company again was?"* or *"Sorry, can you say who you are again please?"*. When asked these kinds of supplementary questions it's really important to maintain your matter of fact demeanor and simply reply briefly with the information and no more.

"Of course, It's Dave Smith, ABC Company calling for John Jones please-Thank you"

You'll see above that by replying like this you've stuck to the straightforward framework and no more.

I keep saying no more, because there's one thing that you may be tempted to do when you're at this point in the conversation, particularly if you're nervous which you're bound to me when you first start making your calls-jump in and start talking! You may feel the pressure to fill the silence or to help the person who has answered your call with more information on the basis that if you give them more information they'll feel better about putting you through but believe me, less is more in telephone marketing and selling, and you only need to be answering what you've been asked when you've been asked it. The danger of starting to talk more is that you may just say something which completely throws a spanner in the works and someone who was just about to press the transfer button on the switchboard will change their mind and you may get asked or meet with any one of the questions/statements below.

I'll be dealing with objections later in the book but for the purposes of dealing with reception/switchboard all I'm going to say is that being straightforward, honest, open and upfront is the best policy. It doesn't mean that you'll get through but remember what I told you earlier in the book, you aren't going to get through every time anyway, and in some cases you'll always get through, even after one of the seemingly challenging questions/statements below so show that you're different. Don't try and navigate your way around the question, just answer it in a ..you've guessed it...straightforward way and you'll make a lot more friends. I've given you some examples of how to answer in each case with a bit of psychology that lies behind the words too.

As you'll see with all the examples of answers I'll give you in this section there's no magic to getting past the question and through to your contact

I've lost count of how many sales books I've read that say things like *"never disclose what your call is about"* or *"never discuss your business with receptionists"* or *"Do whatever you can to get through"*. That frankly is nonsense. I'm not saying you have to give them war and peace, but simply enough to answer their question, and there are a few different ways to do it depending on what they're asking.

In the interests of variety I've given answers here for different products and services:

What's it regarding?

This is probably the most asked questions by receptionists. It's also almost universally interpreted by sales people as being a "blocking" kind of question. Sometimes it is, but equally sometimes it's being asked because the receptionist genuinely wants to help you and make sure what you want to speak about is handled by the person you're asking for.

"Thank you, I was looking for John's feedback on some work we've been delivering recently for other facilities managers in your sector/area, is he in?" - Commercial Cleaning

"Thank you, I was interested to hear John's feedback on the letter I sent to him recently, is he in today?" - Various

"Thank you, that's a good question with a number of answers. I'm conscious of your time, so to keep things brief, I was looking for Jane's feedback in the area of disaster recovery, is she in"

"Thank you, it's just a quick call regarding reducing the Company's fuel bill, is he in?" Vehicle tracking

"Thank you, it's a quick call about air con servicing, not sure if we can help John but I'm sure he'll tell me if we can't, is he in?" - Air Con

There are lots and lots of these. The truth is if you're hit with the *"What's it regarding?"* question as I said above it's either because the person you're speaking with is trying to block you because he/she has been told not to put through any sales calls, or it could be they are simply asking for clarification. So, on the basis of keeping an open mind don't pre judge the reason behind the question, just answer the question and go from there.

The next few questions are ones which receptionists are taught on courses they go on to help them screen out unwanted calls. If you hit any of these, then you're probably dealing with a Company that has "policies" in place for "cold calls". Relax and don't worry. Be straightforward and answer the question.

Does he know you?

This is a good one and a question that many a salesperson has shot themselves in the foot with. The temptation here is of course to say that you do, or that you have met a while ago but he may not remember, or some other version of this. Problem is that your credibility is shot to pieces as soon as you get through because it quickly dawns on your prospect that you haven't in fact met or spoken before and therefore you've tricked your way in-Game over.

"No, I've never met or spoken with him before, I bet that's a refreshingly straightforward answer for you isn't it!, is he in?"

Has he spoken to you before?

"No, not yet, is he in?"

Are you introducing your Company?

When you hear this one in particular it's a very strong indication that you are going to be told that there's a policy in place for introducing yourself which usually revolves around sending an e mail without having had any kind of conversation with your prospect. I'm not saying we should never send introductions by e mail or letter first, in fact as previously covered a strategy of combined direct mail and telemarketing or e broadcast and telemarketing can be hugely effective. I'm just saying that in the instances where you haven't previously sent something then it's far better to have at least a brief initial conversation first . The astute amongst you will have seen that of course when you get through to John you are not going to change horses by not even asking him what he' needs from a prospective supplier, the opposite is true. You'd actually lead with explaining that we'd called to ask him how we can best introduce ourselves etc, you understand that naturally he'll have a criteria for that and you wanted to make sure you're on the right lines before you send anything in. Inevitably a conversation at that point is likely to develop naturally, the result of which could be anything from you setting an appointment, to you actually gaining your prospects agreement that they are happy to receive something further from you (and exactly what they'd like to see) or of course that what you have is not right for them. The point is that you've kept your credibility in tact with what you told the receptionist. If she puts you through in this scenario she will say something along the lines of *"Dave King from ABC is on the line, says he wants to ask you about what you need to see from prospective suppliers"* If you then start with an introduction that doesn't even refer to this you're game will be over before its even started.

So as a way to meet this question head on, here are a few different answers- have fun with them.

"Yes, I am and I wanted to ask John personally what he'd need from me in order to meet his introduction criteria, is he in?"

"Yes, I am, and I wanted to very briefly ask John what information specifically he needs from his point of view in the introduction letter that I'll be sending him, is he in?"

"Yes and I just want to confirm with John briefly exactly what he'd like to see from me in my introduction letter that will be coming opt to him"

Is there anything you can send her?

Another perennial favourite of people that answer the phone on reception. What lies behind the request of course is the hope that you'll just say, yes ok, then maybe be happy with going away with a generic e mail address to send something into which I think we're all agreed isn't the greatest outcome for you. Marginally better could be obtaining your contact's direct e mail address, but again we owe it to ourselves to at least attempt to get through so the following may help you?

"I'd be delighted to send her some information but I know she's a busy lady and the last thing I want to do is clog up her in box with information that's not specific to her situation. I'd like to have a brief word with her to at least make sure that what I send over is of value to her, is she in?"

"Thank you that's a good idea but as what we do is different for each client I'd like to make sure what she receives is relevant and specific to your Company. I'd be able to establish that in about a minute by briefly speaking with her, is she in?"

"I know how much I dislike receiving information that's not relevant so I don't want to get off on the wrong foot by doing that. Ideally I'd be able to have a very brief word just to confirm what she'd need from me to evaluate what we do, is she in?"

And finally...

"That's a great idea, what specific aspect about our service do you feel she'd be most likely to respond to?"

This is really an answer to put your call answerer on the spot a little bit and if they are hesitant you can continue with..

"Apologies, didn't mean to put you on the spot there, if I could grab a quick word with her I'd be able to make sure that what I send across after our conversation is exactly what she needs, is she in?"

Is this a sales call?

This is a response that again suggests you may be up against it a little. Remember, just relax, don't feel challenged or threatened, and just calmly answer the question.

"I certainly wouldn't have thought so, that's not the way we work here, I'm just looking for some feedback, is she in?"

"I'm sorry if I gave you that impression, although I would imagine you do get lots of people calling in to directly sell their services. It's not the way we work here; my call is simply to see from John whether we have some common ground in relation to ...."

"Sorry, when you say sales call what do you mean?" Another "on the spot" question.
If they reply *"Well, you know trying to do business with us"* you can continue with
"I have no idea whatsoever if that will be the case, I'm sure John would let me know if what we do is something on his radar right now, if not no problem, but I can't say without speaking with him, is he in?"

And just to show you that there's no rhyme or reason to all of this I've got through many, many times by saying...

"Yes, it is!, is he in?"

He doesn't take cold calls

"Thank you for letting me know that Jill, I like people being straightforward with me. Can I ask you a question? You are in a position where you get to know how everyone in the business operates. If you wanted to get John's attention about a service that you absolutely knew could help him how would you do it?"

Another "on the spot" question that forces the person to actually put some logic into what they've just told you, namely that you are not going to reach John with a call. So, it's getting them to tell you how *they* would get his attention.

A few final words on receptionists

They are doing their job. Often they may have been on the receiving end of some not particularly pleasant calls so their start position can often be guarded. Never forget that they are your key to getting through. You are never going to win them all but with the right attitude you'll win more than enough to help you build a great business.

Relax, never feel threatened or challenged, be human and genuinely do your best to create some rapport between you, it goes a long way.

Work with the willing, don't try and bash down firmly shut doors, there are plenty out there that will already be slightly open waiting for your call to fully open them.

Have fun with it, smile and relish the challenge!

Call Opening 1 -a variation

An alternative to this opening has a subtle difference and can almost subliminally make the person think that you're talking with that you know the contact you're calling, or at least have had previous conversations with them. Here it is:

"Hello, Good Morning, it's Jill Smith from ABC Company calling for Hannah, (pause) Hannah Evans please-Thank you"

Mentioning your contacts first name with a pause and then stating their full name is again a way of creating the impression that you have dealt with that person before. However, and this is where we are being true to our straightforward philosophy, at no point have you said so (and later on I'll show you how to answer that question should it arise)

My only caveat with this alternative is that it works best when calling smaller companies than larger corporate firms where use of people's full names is more the norm. That said there has been a shift in recent years away from formal business to informal but I'd recommend opening one for corporate and the alternative for SME's, and partnerships.

Alternative language

Making sales calls is all about finding the words that you feel work best for you. I've given you below an alternative opening to try. Use both and measure which one you have more success with

Call Opening 2

"Good morning, it's Dave Smith from ABC Company, would you happen to know if John Jones is in the office today please?"

This opening makes the person actually give some thought to what you've said. You may receive responses like:

"I think so, or I think I saw him earlier let me check for you", or as we've discussed previously you may just be put through.

When you get the response that yes, they believe he is in just continue with:

"OK, that's great, as I say it's Dave Smith from ABC Company, thank you"

Again, your response here is quite assumptive in that you are pre empting them having to ask you again who you are and where you are from, and your "thank you" indicates that you fully expect to be speaking with John Jones.

You will have also noticed again the subtle variation of the way you say your name on this one.

"It's Dave, Dave Smith from ABC Company, thank you"

Opening 2 (Variation)

As with the first opening I'm giving you here a variation which you can call with:

"Good morning, it's Dave Smith from ABC Company, would you happen to know if John, (pause) John Jones is in the office today please?"

As you can see, all we've done is added the contacts first name first followed by a slight pause and then his full name.

The interpretation of your call openings is down to the person who is handling your call.

Although I can assure you that you've stacked the odds in your favour by opening like this, crucially you haven't at any point been anything other than....straightforward.

When your contact isn't available

So what do you do when the receptionist comes back to you and says that sorry but John Jones or Jill Smith isn't available. Little quiz to see if you're getting the hang of this:

A: Say thanks, and you'll call back another time

B: Say thanks and do you know when he'll be available (better but still room for improvement)

Or

C Use the **Straightforward Approach™** response to handling this

Well, nothing wrong in principle or on the face of it with A or B but just think for a minute what the objective of **Straightforward Approach™** is. It's to be easy to follow and easy to do. So if we just leave our call there we're potentially making life harder for ourselves and the receptionist who will be taking our next call because we have to go through the whole process again of calling at a random time in the hope he may be there, then getting put through etc.

Why not do some things now, on this call that will smooth the way for you.

Here they are:

1. Personalise your relationship with the receptionist/ person who picks up your call

Say *"No problem, I appreciate your help. Sorry, I didn't ask your name"*

Most people will be ok with this because hardly any salespeople personalize their relationships with people on reception teams as they don't value their importance, but as I said in an earlier section they can be your best allies.

Let's assume our receptionist replies "Jean, Jean Smith"

2. Identify an optimum time for you to call back

Say to her *"Thanks Jean,...Oh ,before I go I was hoping you could help me. I know that John's schedule is often busy, are you aware of the next time according to the information you have about his movements that he'll definitely or as sure as you can be that John will be in his office."*

She may not know, in which case you've lost nothing. However, she may well know and reply

"Well, he'll definitely be in on Friday 2pm"

3. Obtain a direct dial number for your contact and an e mail address

"Great. And I know how busy your switchboard is Jean too, so could I suggest that I help by making one less call for you to deal with and contact John direct, what's his direct number please?"

This is far more subtle than simply asking for his direct dial number.

"01206 1234 567"

"Thank you, and if I wanted to reach him by e mail, what address would I get him on please?

Again a far more subtle way of asking for your contacts e mail address.

Now, if we're talking poker here, a Royal Flush would be you get to uncover when your contact will be sat at his or her desk, by day and time, what their direct dial number is so you don't have to go via the switchboard, and you're given their e mail address too. In the real world that happens all the time, if you ask in the way I've described, but of course you may draw a blank on all or some of these points.

Obviously if you get the Ace of Diamonds, the direct dial number then your destiny is now in your own hands. I've given you below however what to do in other situations.

If future availability of contact unknown and you are unable to get a direct dial number

No problem, simply say to Jean

"Ok Jean, appreciate your help, I'm sure we'll be speaking again when I call back..Dave Smith ABC Company"

You add your own name and Company again so as to reinforce you in Jean's mind. She'll be impressed with your approach but names can be quickly forgotten which isn't all bad because she may remember your voice, but belt and braces approach says that we cement your name in her mind again.

If future availability is known

"Thank you Jean. Could I ask a favor please? I know you get a lot of calls but I'd be grateful if you could get a note to John to say that I've called today and will be calling back at X at Y as you've suggested"

There's a bit of psychology at play here. By asking Jean to get a message to John saying that you'll be calling back at X at Y as she's suggested what you're doing here is to get Jean involved directly in the process. She's told you to call at a certain time, John Jones will know that you'll be calling back and so when you do call at X on Y on the dot showing complete reliability and professionalism on your part she may feel duty bound to do everything she can to get your call through.

Again, in the real world that happens all the time, but equally you may call back at X at Y and Jean's off ill and the person who is now on reception doesn't want to play ball at all!

But that as they say is the fun of the fair.

What I want you do to is really get to grips with the call approaches and variations I've given you here. Make them your own. Make calls, vary the speed and tone of your voice, try approach 1 then 2, then use the variations and start to get a feel for which approach and language feels most comfortable to you.

Being natural and yourself is the key to this. Relax and have fun with it. Challenge yourself to see how many times you get put through first time using one of the approaches. Do a split test. Call one way one day and then switch over, which one is working best for you.

Think about it like this, we spoke about the three thirds earlier. By becoming good at your call openings you'll be getting through more times than you currently are on the "up for grabs" third. Remember we spoke about those companies where how you come across will dictate whether or not you get through.

Think back to the lifetime value of what one customer is worth to your business in a year. Even if you got through to just 10-20 more people a day what potential revenue impact could that have on your business?

I'll tell you...MASSIVE

So now we're going to move on to the real nitty gritty. What do you say when you're transferred and...don't panic...your decision maker is on the line"!

Where you don't have a name

As you know from an earlier section I the book, more often than not if you've done your homework correctly on the data side of things you will have a named contact to ask for when you call your target Company. However, there are occasions where the named contact may have moved on and the reception team has been reluctant to give you the new contact, often due to a "no name policy". I'll cover how best to deal with that particular little gem later. It may be alternatively that there is a particular company that you've read about or someone has mentioned to you that you'd like to call but you don't have a contact name to ask for. Without doubt it's a million times easier to call when you have a name than not so it's worth spending some time to find one. Fortunately we live in an age where this process is a lot easier than it used to be. The web makes finding contacts within Companies actually pretty easy, and there are several ways to do it. There should never really be a situation where you're having to call a Company without a name. I've set out below some methods that I personally use to find contacts:

Research

1. **Linkedin (www.Linkedin.com)**

   If you're selling a B2B product or service and you're not on Linkedin then you need to register (it's free) and start building your profile straightaway. I'm not even going to attempt to go into in this book how to use Linkedin as a sales tool, it's a whole separate topic and one which I recommend you look into but suffice to say that it's a superb platform for helping to build your business. I'm just going to highlight to you that once you log onto Linkedin you have the facility to run an advanced search for contacts with a particular job title at a particular Company. If you get a direct hit on a job title/Company name search then great. It may be that the contact for your particular job function is not listed but think creatively. If there is a contact with an associated role, even if it's quite a loose connection then you can use them as your first point of contact and ask for their help in directing you to the right person.

   The main thing is that you will have a name to work with on the switchboard as opposed to having to call with the standard:

   "Who is in charge or/responsible for/takes decisions on XYZ "

   This kind of approach immediately flags your call up as a sales call.

2. Google (www.google.com)

Let's say just for an example that you are looking for the Head of Facilities for a Bank, let's call it the Prospect Bank. A bit of creative Googling with the job title and the Bank name may bring up a contact name. If it does make sure they article is reasonable recent otherwise there's a chance that your contact may have moved on in which Case you'll be back to square one.

3. Company Website

Seems obvious but one that a lot of people don't check out. Some Companies have a very useful "Our People" section which tells you the who's who. Again, if your specific job role contact is not listed, then pick someone that's associated and use them as your start point.

Remember that it's human nature to want to help people. When you get through to someone who you know isn't really your contact then just be up front and straightforward in what you're trying to achieve.

"Hello John, I was hoping you could help me please. I understand that you head up ABC at Acme Widgets but I didn't know if that would also cover the area of ABC-Is that something that also falls under your umbrella?"

Some people will tell you straight away that yes it is and how can they help, or no it isn't and if not they'll tell you who you need to speak with, their direct line, e mail address favourite song, food and which football team they support. Some won't, they'll be quite guarded about it all and tell you absolutely nothing, preferring to ask you to e mail a generic e mail address and that "your e mail will be reviewed and if appropriate someone will get back to you" or something similar. The remainder may help you out dependent on how you come across. We're back to the three thirds again. It's worth a try and you have nothing to lose. Remember at all times. Polite, professional, courteous (but not subservient) and under no circumstances get dragged into any kind of conflict. If someone doesn't want to point you in the right direction that is entirely up to them, thank them for their time and get off the phone. You've got plenty more Companies to call.

If you can't find a name through research

If you genuinely can't find a name through research then you have three courses of action open to you. To be frank none are half as effective as calling with a name but both are worth a try. The issue here though is that your call answerer is going to know straight away that your call is from a sales and marketing perspective and you're in their hands as to whether they want to play ball with you.

"Hello, I'd be grateful if you can help me please. I've been asked to find out who is in charge of X for your Company as we'd like to send a letter of introduction/an invite to an event we'll be holding for people in the X sector. Can I ask who I should address that to please?"

If you are given a name here then you've done well so may as well push your luck a little bit:

"That's great, thank you, and if we wanted to contact Jill by telephone to get her feedback afterwards is there a direct line for her?"

If you get that, you must go for the hat trick!:

"Thank you, and just in case we decide to ask for her feedback by e mail instead, what address would I use to reach her?"

The next option takes us right back to old school selling but if it's all you've got left....:

"Good Morning, I'd be grateful if you could help me please. Who is responsible for X at ABC Company please?"

You never know, they might just tell you, in which case whilst you're on the phone you may as well see what other information you can uncover as above.

The final approach in this section involves asking to speak not with a decision maker as such but a senior PA or secretary within a business. You will need to at least know who the very top executive in a Company is, MD, CEO, Chairman etc. Now it's not these people we want to speak with it's their PA.

"Good Morning, it's James Smith from Acme Widgets, could I go through to Mr. Johnson's (MD for example) PA please-thank you"

I've generally found PA's, however senior, to be quite accessible, and helpful. They know who's who and what's what in an organisation. Once through, listen carefully as they more often than not announce their name first. Continue with:

"Good morning Jill, I'd be grateful if you could help me please. I understand that you're the PA to Mt Johnson the MD?"

"Yes, that's right"

"Excellent, I'm in the right place! It wasn't Mr. Johnson that I wanted to speak with actually but I thought you would be the best person to point me in the right direction for whoever it is that heads up X for the Company. Who do you think I'd be best speaking with about that?"

I've had various responses to this one ranging from getting the name, direct dial, e mail address and being transferred directly to the person I need, through to sorry Robbie, It's not really my place to give you that information so I'll have to put you back to the switchboard"

Doesn't matter, it's always worth the effort to make the call and see where it takes you.

The two phase system for when you don't have a name

If you've been successful in obtaining a name with either of the three approaches above I have one final tip for you. Quit while you're ahead. Don't go on to ask to actually ask to speak with the contact. That can wait for another day(unless of course you are offered the opportunity to speak with them straight away which sometimes happens even if you call with the "want to send in a letter/invite approach". I've had it where I'm given the name and then the next thing that happens is I'm being put through. This can happen because the reception team is almost on auto pilot. They hear your words but their actions are automatic and they hit the transfer button)

The main objective has been achieved. You now have a name to work with. Leave it a few days or so and call back. Phase one get the name, phase two call back.

More advanced methods

The options above should suffice in the majority of cases to help you at least get a name within an organization. As I said, the web is a mine of information and sometimes you can even find people's direct dial numbers publicly available. Always screen them though through a CTPS checking service to make sure it's ok to call. If you're ever asked how you came by a number that you've sourced yourself just say that you were provided it by your research team.

There are some more advanced methods for reaching people within organizations where either you've been blocked at reception level, so in other words you have a name but just can't get through, or you don't have a contact name and need to find someone in that department.

If you're blocked at reception when you have a name.

Go onto the Company website, or Google and look for an alternative contact number within that Company/ Organization. It doesn't really matter what department it is as basically you're going to be asking whoever picks up the phone to transfer you. Let's assume in this case the person we want to speak with is Dave Smith in Facilities but we've been blocked by reception. This is how you do it.

Call your alternative number and when you get through, just say:

"I do apologise, I've misdialed somewhere along the line, I was actually looking to speak with Dave, Dave Smith in Facilities, sorry to be a pain are you able to transfer me please, thank you?"

Now, in my experience many people are only too happy to help you, will have a bit of a laugh about it, and just put you through. As with all things some won't and will want to know more, just keep it as brief as you can without sounding too cagey. It's worth a go, you have nothing to lose.

Auto switchboards

Many Companies operate automatic switchboards. If you're calling into a Company without a name but you do know the specific department you need, let's say Marketing. There's another approach you can try that's similar to the one above. You can call the main number, select a department other than the one you need and then when someone picks up and says *"Sales"* or *"Accounts"* or *"Post Room"* or whatever it is, you can say:

"I do apologise, I've hit the wrong option there, it was actually Marketing I wanted, are you able to transfer me please?"

Just as they transfer you:

"Thank you, oh sorry before I go through, who heads up marketing these days?"

You'll find with this one that people who work in sales departments will be particularly helpful in getting you to the right person. It's that "we're in the same game" thing at play.

Worth a go.

Paralysis By Analysis- A word of caution

As with all things it's easy to get side-tracked by "research". If you're not careful you can end up spending more time researching than calling. I've worked with sales people in the past who use the shield of research to hide them from the reality of getting on the phone and calling people. Absolutely, if you want to call a specific Company and you don't have a name then by all means spend a bit of time trying to find one quickly. If you can then great, if not move on, you will always have plenty more people to call.

Chapter 6

Alternative call approaches, call plans, and developing the conversation

Once you are through to your decision maker contact

I'll tell you now, that it is completely normal to feel a little surge or adrenalin when you get through to your decision maker, especially when you are finding your feet with your prospecting. In fact even people who've been working the phone for years will tell you if they're being honest that they still get that when making some calls. However, the key to this is to stay as calm and relaxed once you're through as you were when speaking with Jean! Earlier in the book I spoke about feeling pressure to perform when making phone calls, and believe me pressure is one thing you really don't need to be giving yourself. Remember you will always have loads of people to call so your business success does not rest with this one, or any one single phone call. You are calling to see if you can help. Plain and simple. If you can great. If you can't great. If you maybe can, that's ok too. It's simply a fact finding mission.

Whatever the outcome here it's a win all the way for you. Your straightforward approach and style will be welcomed by the people you're calling. People respond in kind. Call like a scripted Dalek and you'll be treated like one. Call in a human way, but above all in a straightforward way and people in the main will be straightforward with you too.

Call Approach 1

"Good Afternoon John, I was hoping that you could help me please. My names Dave Smith from ABC Company, we've not spoken before but I understand that anything to do with X would be overseen by you, is that right?"

The reason that we tell John and are quite up front about the fact we have not spoken with him before is that often decision makers are used to sales people disguising the real reason for their call behind some kind of reference to a previous meeting somewhere or alluding to the fact that they have spoken before in some way. **Straightforward Approach™** is built on being completely up front right from the off.

It also helps the person you are speaking with because if you aren't straightforward about this they can be spending the first few seconds of the call trying to fathom out where you're from, where you know them from etc which can be off putting for them and you.

So this deals with the first question that goes through a prospects mind when you get through to them:

"Who is this, and where do I know them from/they know me from?"

You'll notice also that you will be saying "anything to do my X would be overseen by you, is that right?"

This is intentionally instead of saying *"I understand that any decisions on X are taken by you, is that right?"* This is because bringing the word "decisions" into the conversation is far too traditional and salesy. It's a word salespeople use..decisions. Let's be frank about it, if we've done our homework on our prep phase we know it's them that take decisions for X, and so we don't at this stage need to bring that up. That isn't to say that we won't cover it later on but not now, and even when we do, we won't be asking it like that.

Other ways to say it....

Remember, our approach is about being human and natural. So if saying *"I understand that anything to do with X would be overseen by you, is that right?"* doesn't feel right to you, how else could you say it whilst keeping the meaning?

How about *"I understand that anything to do with X would fall under your umbrella, is that right?"*

Or *"I understand as far as X is concerned John, everything needs to be discussed with you, is that right?"*

Or *"I understand that you head up X there, is that right?"*

Or *"I understand that you're responsible for X is that right?"*

Bottom line is that we're simply looking to confirm that our homework is correct, and in vast majority of cases it will be.

Quick point here though. In the same way that you are going to grab their attention in a short while with what you do, you can warm them up for that by grabbing their attention with what they do!

For example instead of saying:

"I understand that anything to do with facilities is overseen by you, is that right?"

Why not say:

"I understand that anything to do with the smooth running of the building is overseen by you, is that right?"

Instead of:

"I understand that anything to do with cleaning is overseen by you is that right?"

Why not say:

"I understand that anything to do with ensuring the very best working environment for staff, is overseen by you, is that right?"

What you're doing here is early on in the call showing the person you're calling that you understand the importance of their job.

I've had lots of people come back to me when I've "re framed" their job role and say *"that's a good way to put it, I like that"* or *"I've never heard anyone put it like that before"*

Be different.

Why ask for help in your approach?

There's some simple psychology at play here. It's human nature to want to help people if they ask for help. Even if a prospect doesn't on a conscious level realize it, they will practically find it more difficult (although not impossible!) to be confrontational with you at this point. It's almost a subliminal message that connects with their very basic level human instinct. It humanizes you in the mind of the prospect.

Contact confirms you're talking to the right person

So now, let's assume that you're through and your contact has confirmed that you're talking to the right person, how do we move things along from there? This is a really important part of the call. Think about it like this, you've done your homework on your target Company, you have successfully got put through by reception and there they are so to speak, they're on the line. I want you to write the following word on a big piece of card and have it on your desk when making your calls and the word is Relax. Like I said, it's natural to feel a bit nervous at this point but the less you transmit your nerves down the phone line the better. If you relax, generally people will relax with you. The more natural, human and real you are the more people respond in kind. That said, you are going to have to have a compelling reason for your prospect to want to carry on speaking with you. I can tell you however that if you've delivered your qualification in terms of confirming that your prospect is in fact the right person to talk about regarding X and they have engaged with you along the lines of *"Yes, that's right, or yes that's me"* you will have already placed yourself in front of many stereotypical cold callers who by their very nature in their approach tick the wrong boxes in the mind of the person they're calling, and instead of a confirmation from their prospect as above, will instead often get something like *"Yes, but what's this all about, or yes, but I don't have time to talk"*, or their tone is such that it's pretty clear that the conversation hasn't got off to a good start. This is because as we've looked at before people make very quick decisions about you on the telephone and if there's anything in your opening that sets off alarm bells your prospect will head your call off at the pass before it's even got going. Conversely, well delivered your opening can often get your prospect to relax and lighten up a bit and it's not uncommon at all to get things at this point like *"For my sins, yes"*, or *"Amongst many other things, yes"* or *"That's one of the hats I wear"* or even a playful *"Who told you that. It's just a rumour!"* and my favorite of all *"I could tell you, but I'd have to kill you"* These are all examples of real life responses to the qualifying opening of a call I've made and a good indication that I was speaking with someone who's happy to let the call develop. There's nothing like good rapport or chemistry to oil the wheels of the telephone sales process so look to create it at every opportunity.

The X Factor and why do you need it

It's because to get the person's attention you'll need to have the X Factor! The X Factor being a very good reason for them to continue to listen with interest to what you have to say. So you need to make it good, otherwise however well things have gone up to this point they'll be reaching for the big red button.

The second thing therefore that is going through a prospects mind is:

"What's in this for me?"

They need to be satisfied that what you have is going to be of benefit, can help them solve an issue and importantly is worthy of a few minutes of their time. Time is a commodity that no one has much of so you need to have an overwhelming reason for someone to allocate a few of their very precious minutes to your call.

Here is an pneumonic to help you remember what your prospect has going through their mind when you get through to them.

W hats

I n

T his

F or

M e

An X Factor statement, or sometimes what I refer to as being an infomercial is something that demonstrates to your prospect that you understand their world in terms of issues that they are dealing with in their role, and that importantly you have been helping other people with those very same issues.

So before I get into the language aspects of the X Factor part of your call, I want to ask you a question:

What is the major headache that your product or service solves for the person you're speaking with? I don't mean what does your product or service do, but what is the major headache that your product or service solves.

So many people can rattle off 50 things that their product or service is or does but I have some news for you. No one is interested. No one is interested in what your product or service is or does, they are only interested in what your product or service does FOR THEM. What problem, issue, and headache it solves to make their life easier. In other words you need to be selling the benefits of what you have and not the features.

FAB

In order to help you craft your X Factor statement I'm going to just give you some examples of the difference between Features and Benefits.

Features are what something is or has and a benefit is what that feature actually does for your prospect which will make their life easier, help them solve an issue, make them more money, reduce costs, operate more efficiently etc.

Examples:

Feature - *"Our pen has a nib that is guaranteed not to leak"*

Benefit Statement- *"Our pen has a nib that is guaranteed not to leak which means that you can confidently place it inside the jacket pocket of your suit in the knowledge it will never cause a stain"*

Feature – *"Our cleaners use only the latest eco friendly products"*

Benefit Statement – *"Our cleaners use only the latest high quality eco friendly products which means that not only will your floors and office furniture look absolutely pristine at all times, but you'll also benefit from contributing to your Company's reduction in your carbon footprint"*

Feature – *"This computer monitor uses 20% less energy than a standard one"*

Benefit Statement –*"This computer monitor uses 20% less energy than a standard one which means that by installing these across your workstations you'll be saving a considerable amount of money across the office, enabling you to invest it in other areas"*

Just remember that to turn a feature into a benefit you need to use the words:

"Which means that"

Now clearly to accurately craft an X Factor statement you are going to have to put yourself in the shoes of the person you're calling. Think about what major headaches they are facing in their job role and start crafting statements that will grab their attention. The example below are ones that I use when making calls for Calls That Count:

"We work with Sales and Marketing Directors throughout the UK helping them by generating more sales appointments and leads for their sales team, which means that by working with us they can focus more of their valuable time on warm qualified prospects"

"We work with Sales and Marketing Directors providing their sales teams with a steady flow of new sales appointments and leads which means that by working with us they can get on with focusing on warm prospects and increasing sales revenues in the knowledge the all important prospecting is being taken care of"

Spend some time doing this and you should be able to come up with 10 or more ways to get your compelling statement across.

To help, just ask what is/are the major headache (s) this person is facing, and what benefit do we provide that takes that headache away.

The idea of the X Factor statement, or infomercial also known as a "hook" is to deliver just enough to grab the attention but not in any way at all to start selling what you do.

Practice your statements over and over and over so that they become second nature to you.

Then practice the call plan right from the start:

Example:

"Good Afternoon John, I was hoping you could help me please, my names Robbie Stepney from Calls That Count, we've not spoken before, but I understand that anything to do with generating additional sales revenue for the Company is overseen by you, is that right?"

"Yes"

"That's great thanks. Just a very straightforward call. We work with Sales and Marketing Directors throughout the UK helping them by generating more sales appointments and leads for their sales team, which means that by working with us they can focus more of their valuable time on warm qualified prospects"

Check this is a good time to talk-you can't be serious!

Yes, I am. After you've delivered your X Factor attention grabbing statement I'm now going to tell you to do something that goes against pretty much any other sales training material I've ever seen or heard. You're going to check with your prospect that this is a good time to talk. If you told an "old school" sales person that you're going to ask your prospects whether it's a good time to talk they would faint! Reason is that they would say to you that gives the prospect an opportunity to say no it isn't and you've lost your opportunity to sell to them. I say, hang on that's rubbish. First of all if you've delivered a good infomercial attention grabbing statement and your prospect genuinely has the time to talk they will do, because it is relevant and beneficial for them to do so. Only reason they wouldn't is if it genuinely isn't convenient to talk, and I'll deal with that in a second. The only other reason for them saying that no it isn't a good time to talk is because they really aren't that interested in what you have called about and for many people saying that it's not a good time to talk is more diplomatic than saying that no they are not interested in talking. So, guess what, that's right I'll show you how to flush out those people too.

So, first of all this is how we check that we've called at a good time to talk.

Straight after your infomercial, say:

"Can I just check, are you ok to talk briefly?"

Other ways to say it:

"Can I just check, is this a good time to talk briefly"

"Can I just check with you John that it's a convenient time to talk briefly"

The *"briefly"* is important because it infers that your call is not going to last too long, which when you're first through to someone is far better than them wondering just how long it's all going to take.

The point here is that very few people ever get asked by salespeople whether it's a good time to talk. Salespeople generally assume that it's ok to completely launch into a pitch without any regard for what the other person may have been doing before they called. You don't want to be speaking with someone who is distracted by something else so far better to check.

A lot of people you will call will actually be quite taken back that you've asked them if it's convenient to talk and over the years I've had lots of people actually comment on the fact how nice it is to be asked.

So your call plan now looks like this:

"Good Afternoon John, I was hoping you could help me please , my names Robbie Stepney from Calls That Count, we've not spoken before, but I understand that anything to do with generating additional sales revenue for the Company is overseen by you, is that right?

"Yes, that's me"

"That's great. Just a very straightforward call. We work with Sales and Marketing Directors throughout the UK helping them by generating more sales appointments and leads for their sales team, which means that by working with us they can focus more of their valuable time on warm qualified prospects"

"Can I just check though, is this a good time to talk briefly?"

"Sure, Robbie go ahead"

When you ask if it is a good time to talk it's important that you don't sound apologetic, subservient or unsure of yourself in any way. The words must be delivered in a calm but assumptive way, like you fully expect your prospect to say that it's fine. The psychology behind the question is not to convey that you think that your prospect may not want to talk with you and that's why you're asking, but rather it's purely you being professional enough to respect their time and have the confidence to give the decision as to whether the conversation continues to them.

The inflection in your voice needs to go down at the end of this question, and definitely not up as is common in an Australian accent for example. Upward inflection in your voice in a sales situation is often perceived as being uncertainty on your part and at all times you should be conveying that you have complete certainty about what you're saying and importantly what your product/service can do for your prospect.

If they say it isn't a good time to talk

This is not a problem, and could mean one of two things. It can be that the person you've called is interested in talking further with you but they simply don't have the time to discuss it right now in which case it would be a good idea for you to establish a good time to call them back and when you do you have a warm call not a cold call. Call backs wherever possible should be dated and timed and not lefty open ended like *"tomorrow, or next week"* The second reason for someone saying that it's not a good time to talk is as I said earlier a polite way of saying to you that they don't want to talk with you. Your job is to get to the bottom of which case you are dealing with.

A good way to do that is:

"That's ok, can I ask John. I'm happy to call you back but to save you time only if in principle you feel that this is something that you'd be happy to talk further about, but equally no problem if it isn't, I'll be guided by you on that"

Straightforward isn't it. Essentially you're putting the ball in their court and letting them decide what happens from here. People are not used to sales people relinquishing control, they are more used to salespeople trying to exert control but believe me it's a very powerful thing to do to place the control as to what happens next firmly in the hands of your prospect. It subliminally says to them that you are ok with whatever way this goes and have the confidence to be that way.

Interesting things happen in sales when you give people the impression that far from being hell bent on selling furiously what you have to offer you're actually quite relaxed about it and only want your prospect to talk further with you if they feel it's beneficial for them to do so, and here's the key-they and not you will be the judge of that.

Your prospect will either say that yes it is something they are happy to talk further about in which case you can set a telephone appointment by saying:

"Great, I'm sure your days are always hectic John, what's going to be the best day and time for me to call you so we don't play telephone tennis?"

If you get any other reaction it's likely that you're dealing with the second scenario.

I'll be dealing with handling objections later in the book for the purposes of this section if you feel that your prospect is giving you the brush off, they probably are so end the call with:

"That's fine John. Based on what you've explained to me can I suggest that we leave this one here, but I appreciate your time-Thank-you"

Again you're making life easy for your prospect to retreat from the conversation without any awkwardness on their part or either of you being dragged into the perennial chasing game for no reason.

I estimate that literally billions of pounds worth of time would be saved worldwide if buyers and sellers were completely up front and straightforward with each other. The chasing game is a waste of everyone's time, and time is money.

Work with the willing

I'm a firm believer in working with the willing. Spend your time with people who are demonstrating that they are as keen to work with you as you are with them. Yes, of course people are going to have to make sure that your product or service meets their needs, budget and timescales but you will get to recognize the ones who are moving through your sales process with you in a collaborative way rather than it feeling like you're pulling teeth. Always remember that there are more people out there than you could ever do business with so don't waste time on people who make your life difficult. Be polite and professional at all times but if you ever sense on a phone call that you're not working with the willing and someone is making your life difficult intentionally, diplomatically end your call and move on.

I'm going to be frank with you. Anyone who gets hostile with you for any reason when you've called in the low key, respectful, polite, and professional way that **Straightforward Approach™** advocates, really isn't worth your time. Step back from the call and move on. Often these people would run a mile if they had to make a sales call themselves and their hostility is some sort of defense mechanism.

Here's a way you can determine on a call if you're working with the willing:

Are they being **REAL**

R Responsive to your approach, or unresponsive offering you very little by the way of conversation

E Engaging in conversation with you, or is the conversation as much fun as a visit to the dentist

A Allowing you the space to outline the benefits of what you have to offer, or do they keep interrupting and throwing spanner after spanner in the works

L Listening with interest, or clearly distracted by something else.

More on difficult people later, and how to deal with them.

Before we ,look at how we progress our call once we have been told it's ok to talk just a word about what to do should our prospect tell us that we need to talk with someone else as it isn't them that oversees/is in charge of X.

We're through to the wrong person

Not a problem at all. What we do here is to use the contact we're speaking with to transfer us to the right person.

Just say *"Apologies John, who would be the best person for me to speak with please?"* Then ask if they are able to transfer you directly.

If they aren't able to or don't want to simply thank them for their time and put your phone down.

Then re dial reception and say *"I was just speaking with John Jones, he's suggested that I speak with Ian Brown, please, thank you"*

Of course if you are able to get them to transfer you straight away it's more favorable than having to go back to the switchboard.

You'll have recognized that you have added your *"Please and Thank You"* here.

I'll be showing you later how you can work your way around a switchboard to get to exactly who you need to speak with by enlisting the help of people within the target Company.

Progressing the call-ask a strong opening question

Once you've been given the ok that it's convenient to talk you need to keep the momentum going. You've done really well so far, and the question you ask at this point can be the clincher in terms of being able to make real progress.

Open Questions

Your question really needs to get your prospect to think and respond. The way to do this is ask an open ended question, that is to say one that cannot be answered with a yes or no answer. There are occasions as you'll see later when what are called closed questions, ones that generally meet with a yes or a no answer can help you in the sales process but this is not the time to ask one.

Here is a list of words which will help you to make sure you're asking an open question.

What

Why

When

How

Where

Who

Continue into your open question

Here's how I'd lead into an open question when making calls for my own Company's services just to demonstrate the structure:

"Ok thanks I've given you a call today specifically to ask, how are you currently going about making sure that your sales teams' diaries are full of new appointments?"

Or

"Ok thanks, I've called today specifically to learn more about what types of sales training the Company provides to develop the sales team's phone confidence"

Your leading open question or statement needs to focus their mind on the key issue, headache, problem, or situation that your product/service holds the solution for.

Specifically is a great word, it gives the impression that you know your stuff, and you don't want to waste their time, or yours.

Here are some other examples for different industries:

IT Support
"Ok thanks, I've given you a call today specifically to ask what systems do you currently have in place to ensure that you have an absolute minimum of downtime on your IT network?"

Corporate vehicle leasing
"Ok thanks, I've given you a call today specifically to ask, how do you currently go about making sure you are getting the very best deals available to you for your vehicle fleet renewals?"

Commercial cleaning

"Ok thanks, I've given you a call today specifically to ask when you're evaluating companies as potential suppliers of your cleaning services what are the three main things you look for in them?

Putting it all together

"Good Afternoon John, I was hoping you could help me please, my names Robbie Stepney from Calls That Count, we've not spoken before, but I understand that anything to do with generating additional sales revenue for the Company is overseen by you, is that right?

"Yes, that's me"

"That's great thanks. Just a very straightforward call. We work with Sales and Marketing Directors throughout the UK helping them by generating more sales appointments and leads for their sales team, which means that by working with us they can focus more of their valuable time on warm qualified prospects"

"Can I just check though, is this a good time to talk for a moment?"

"Sure, Robbie go ahead"

"Ok thanks, I've given you a call today specifically to ask, how are you currently going about making sure that your sales teams' diaries are full of new appointments?"

So you've asked your first open question which I'm going to show you how to build upon to develop a conversation, but now is the time for you to listen. There's an old saying that says that we've got two ears and one mouth and we should you use them in that ratio. Unfortunately though many sales people forget and talk far too much and listen far too little. The result is that they miss really useful golden nuggets of information that they are being given. It's these golden nuggets of information that later on in the conversation will enable you to move the call along in the direction you want it to go in. So here's a tip. Once you've asked a question, don't just listen but listen actively.

ACTIVE listening

A Always focus intently on what the person is saying and not on what you want to say next! We all know people who we'll be talking to and we can tell that they are really just waiting for us to finish what we're saying so that they can carry on talking, and that's really irritating. In the same way people pick up very easily if you are not paying attention to what they're saying and are only interested in your own agenda and pitch. A good way to make sure that you don't jump in is to physically put a hand over your mouth when your prospect is talking. Another way is to have a post it note in front of you that says "Ask a question and then SHUT UP", or "2 ears 1 mouth"

C Conversation is key. You don't want to be jumping in and interrupting but we do want to let the other person know we're involved and engaging with what they're saying. So, little acknowledgements like" Uh huh, ok, I see, mmm, that's interesting, all help to keep things in conversation mode.

T Take notes. One of the tools of the trade you'll have on your desk is an A4 lined pad and a pen. Take note of anything that your prospect says that is clearly very important from their point of view. It's easy for notes to get untidy when you're trying to also listen to what someone is saying. A simple method is to just draw a series of rectangles on your sheet of paper and put one point of importance in each one. If something strikes you as being either really important to the person you're speaking to or is something they say that you know will give you some great ammunition to go back on as it highlights a strong benefit of your product or service, simply draw a downwards arrow on top of that box. That way you know by simply glancing at your pad which are the most important points.

I If in doubt clarify. At a suitable pause in your prospects conversation flow it's a good idea to ask them to clarify anything you're not sure of. This is a good thing to do for two reasons. Firstly it makes sure that you get your facts straight but also it highlights that you are taking the time and effort to genuinely understand their situation.

V Voice match. Voice matching is a big topic that goes well beyond the scope of this book but broadly speaking means trying to mirror the tone and pace of the person's voice you're speaking with. People like to talk with people they feel are similar to them. All I'm going to say on this here is that if you're talking with someone who's quite low key they will not respond well if you're being overly bouncy, or "up" in your voice. Equally if you're speaking with a bit of a live wire try to match their energy level and tone as they'll respond better to that as they can relate to it and will see you as being like them.

E Empathise. People will respond better to you if they feel that you are putting yourself in their shoes. If your prospect talks about something that they say for example makes them angry, the empathize with phrases like *"I can understand that" "Yes, I can see why you say that".* Again it's just about being real and human.

Personality Types

Knowledge as they say is power. It's helpful if you can identify early on in a conversation what kind of personality you're dealing with on the phone. If you can, you'll be in a position to voice match better, ask better questions and use language that they'll relate to.

There are 4 main personality types and in reality we are all a mixture of them but typically will have one main one with a secondary one.

ACTOR/EXPRESSIVE- Extrovert, talk a lot, can be quite loud, like to talk about themselves, their businesses, laugh a lot, it's often all about them, like being the centre of attention, often funny, likeable, charismatic. Not too keen on detail, like to see the big picture.

You will enjoy speaking with these people but you'll need to reign them in a bit to keep things on track. Bit of ego massaging doesn't go amiss with these people.

DOER/DOMINANT– Direct, like getting to the point. No time for small talk, like to be in charge. Can speak in quite short staccato sentences, don't suffer fools gladly. Want to know the facts, what's in it for them, what's the bottom line. Their mantra is very much "Let's get on with it".

You will sometimes feel like these types of people are putting you on the spot. Don't get flustered, they're like it with everybody! Keep things to the point, be direct, give them the facts and ask for what you want, don't beat around the bush. Don't feel the pressure to fall into any kind of subservient role in your conversations with these people. Stand your ground, they're often really nice people underneath the hard front that they feel they have to portray.

THINKER/ANALYTICAL- Introvert, wants to consider things carefully, look at the evidence, don't like to be rushed. Like to look at the figures, consult others, reach decisions in their own time.

You will need to give these people the room they need to think. You'll sometimes have long pauses in conversations with thinkers but don't worry about it or feel the need to fill the space. They are thinking. Let them think. You'll need to be quite low key with these people. They like facts and figures and for you to be able to back what you say with hard evidence for them to think about!

FRIEND/WARM- Very nice people! Will be happy to chat with you all day long if you let them. Will rarely challenge what you say but don't mistake that for being the same as them agreeing with what you say. Can sometimes give the impression that they are easy to sell to, but don't ever fall into the trap of thinking that these people are not completely switched on and with it in every way. Whereas the Doer/Dominant type can have a softer more friendly side underneath (if you can get them to be themselves instead of playing a role) the friend/warm type can often have a steely resolve lurking behind the unassuming exterior which enables them to be successful business people.

You'll need to take charge in these conversations and lead the call. These people can often have you ending up in the chasing game if you're not careful as they don't like to say no.

A full explanation of personality types and how best to sell to them is outside the scope of this book. Don't get obsessed with it, just be aware that not everyone is the same. See if you can have a bit of a game and some fun when you're on your calls identifying which type of personality you're dealing with. Play around with matching your voice, tone, and words with theirs and you'll start to find that you can have a conversation with anyone.

I've already mentioned voice matching but another tip is to use the same language as they do. If someone describes something as being brilliant use the word brilliant back, People can relate and warm to people who they perceive to be like them.

Maintaining momentum

Time to fact find, clarify and probe with more open questions

So, you've asked your prospect a question and they've started to answer you. You've taken notes and the first part of the conversation is reaching a natural conclusion. How do we maintain momentum? Easy, we ask more open ended questions to dig a bit deeper. This is how you do it. If you've made notes in the way I suggested you'll have some really good ammunition to go back with. Pick your first point that you've highlighted in your notes and say:

*"Ok, I see, interesting that you mentioned needing a 24 hour response time on service issues, **why** do you feel that is important to you"*

Or

*"When you said that your current provider has let you down a bit recently, **what** did you mean by that?"*

Or

*"You said that you ask potential suppliers to re contact you in good time for the tender process, **when** does that take place, and **what's** the process?"*

Or

*"I understand completely about needing to run any new ideas past your colleagues, **who** else is involved in the process, and **what** roles do they play?"*

Or

*"You said that price is your main criteria for assessing new suppliers but **how** important alongside that are issues such as service and reliability?"*

Or

*"You said that you're always open to seeing what else is available to you in the market, **where** is there room for improvement in your current contract?"*

Or

*"If you were to consider an alternative office supplies Company, **what** are the top things you'd list as being absolute must have's for you even to look more closely at them?"*

The idea here is to simply keep the conversation going by asking more open ended questions and uncovering more deeper level information on the points that you picked up as being key points in their initial response.

For Calls That Count for example, one of my probing questions is:

*"You said that the team is pretty busy right now with appointments which is great, but **what** percentage of their working week is still available to sit in front of more customers?"*

You are not simply asking questions here for the sake of it. You're asking questions that better help you to understand their situation and therefore whether you're able to help them or not (you can't help everyone, and nor should you try to force the issue with people who clearly don't want or have a need for your product/service) By asking good questions you'll also be helping your prospect to better understand how what you have could well benefit them too.

Putting it all together and now adding some open ended questions to fact find, clarify and probe

"Good Afternoon John, I was hoping you can help me please. My names Robbie Stepney from Calls That Count, we've not spoken before, but I understand that anything to do with generating additional sales revenue for the Company is overseen by you, is that right?

"Yes, that's me"

"That's great thanks. Just a very straightforward call. We work with Sales and Marketing Directors throughout the UK helping them by generating more sales appointments and leads for their sales team, which means that by working with us they can focus more of their valuable time on warm qualified prospects"

"Can I just check though, is this a good time to talk for a moment?"

"Sure, Robbie go ahead"

"Ok thanks, I've given you a call today specifically to ask how are you currently generating new sales appointments and leads for your sales team?"

"Well we do lots of things like e broadcasts to get new enquiries, send out brochures and of course we have enquiries via our website, so they're pretty busy at the moment I'm pleased to say"

"I see, that's interesting, you mentioned that they're pretty busy at the moment, how many people do you have on the sales team?"

"We've got 6 but we're also looking to add to that"

"That's interesting, what percentage of your sales team's time is spent in any one week sitting in front of potential clients?"

"Hard to say"

"What about ballpark figure, what would you say?"

"60%"

"I see, and how many more people are joining the team?"

"Probably 3 more in a few months' time"

"Busy time for you then John, out of curiosity, how many of your sales team currently pick up the phone every day to make their own appointments?"

"They all do, but not for long as they're busy looking after our existing clients, sorting out proposals, and dealing with any incoming enquiries"

"What impact does it have on your sales pipeline when the sales team get side-tracked on other things?"

"That's simple. We notice a dip in sales until they get going again"

I could keep adding the dialogue above with more and more questions and in doing so I'd be uncovering more and more really useful ammunition that I'd be able to use as a lever to reach my objective of getting in to see someone.

All I want you to realize up to this point is that good questions about your prospects situation will make your life very easy when it comes to giving them some really great reasons as to why they should meet with you, talk further with you, receive something from you, come to your event, or whatever your objective for the call is.

Remember though, asking a good question is pointless if you don't listen to the answer!

Your aim should be to ask natural questions that are based on information your prospect is giving you. It shouldn't at any point feel like an interrogation, so make your questions flow by changing the pitch and pace of your voice. Contrary to popular belief you do not need to be word perfect and there's no problem at all in tripping over your words sometimes and having to re ask the question, or even including the odd "filler" noise like an "um" or an "er" because that just shows you to be human. The most confident well informed articulate people in the world "um and er" sometimes so relax and don't worry about it. I'm giving you permission to do it. You are not a robot.

Practice how many different ways you can ask the same question. Try playing around with the order of the words. Change the start of the question. Substitute a *"That's interesting"* for an *"Interesting you should say that".*

Also play around with how you give your X Factor statement, see how "matter of fact" and flowing you can make it, in other words although I'm giving you the language in **Straightforward Approach™** you need to make it your own.

Asking your prospect what impact not doing something is having on their business is a very powerful thing to do because it encourages them to voice their own concerns about the situation. Think of ways with your own product and service that you can get your prospect to focus on the impact not doing something or where something is being done but not to a high enough standard is having on their business.

As an example for an IT Support Company, an impact question could be *"What potential impact do you think not having a fast response IT Support service could have in the event of a major fault?"*

For a book keeper *"What impact does not having all your books straight have on you and your business?"*

Your job is to focus your prospects mind on what they are missing out on, leaving themselves open to, potential issues they are storing up, opportunities they are missing.

Summarising and commitment

It's important that you demonstrate to your prospect that you have listened carefully to what they've said, and importantly that you understand what they've said. If you haven't, or you don't you're going to find it difficult to move things along. Sometimes you'll think that you've got a good grasp of someone's situation and what the important things are from their perspective but in reality you haven't. This is particularly true when you're new to calling. Your focus can be on what you're about to say next rather than on what your prospect is saying and you miss things, important things. By summarising and committing your prospect you're giving yourself a chance to correct misunderstandings that you have about what they've told you.

This is how it works:

"John, I've been listening carefully to what you've said and if I understand you correctly, you're mainly unhappy with your current

cleaning Company because their time keeping is poor which leads to issues with areas not being cleaned within the allotted time, is that right?"-Commercial cleaning example

"Jane from what I'm understanding here, your main priority is to reduce each departments overall spend on stationery and at the same time have an ordering system that minimises wastage, is that right?"-Stationery example

"Dave, have I got this right so far. The main priority for you is the have the flexibility to use service engineers purely on an as required basis rather than being tied into any kind of long term contract, is that correct?" - Building maintenance example

The response you're looking for when you put your summary to you prospect is something along the lines of *"Yes, that's it"*, or *"Exactly"* If you get anything other than that or you sense some hesitation in your prospects voice then don't move on at this stage, you need to dig deeper and find out what lies behind the hesitation. If you don't, it will seriously put a spanner in your works when you want to move the call along further.

Reactions similar to these should act as warning signals to you not to move on yet, and the need to qualify more.

"Yes, sort of" "More or less, Yes" "You could put it that way I guess" "You have most of it right, yes"

So here are a few ways you can dig deeper:

"When you say sort of, what am I missing?" "When you say more or less, what have I missed out?" "When you say I have most of it right, what have I missed out or misunderstood?"

As always use your own words to make this more natural for you, but whatever way you do it don't move on until you have the real picture of how your prospect views the situation.

With clarifying things again like this you'll uncover some real gems of information that will help you.

The Qualifiers

So by this stage you will have had a really good conversation with your prospects and gained a thorough understanding of what their issues are. You will also know with some certainty that based on what they've told you, you are in a position to help them. All looking great then isn't it. Well, maybe, but there are three burning questions that they need to answer before you can get onto the home stretch. Simply put they are:
Do they want to be helped? If so, by when? Finally, if you could demonstrate that you're the Company to help them, do they want to talk further? (although this is not of course how we will ask them)

In sales you can end up having some fantastic conversations with people where everything just seems to click. Your prospects situation matches perfectly the solutions that your product or service can solve, you're getting on well but the bottom line is that even though they may appear to be a great match for you in reality they will never turn into a customer. So, how can that be? Quite simple really, they don't see solving the issue as a priority.

The first qualifying question is designed to simply find out whether their situation is one that they *want* to change.

Here are a couple of examples of how to answer the first qualifier:

"John, when you said that you would like to reduce spend on security by 10% over the next year, is that a priority for you?"

Or

"Jane, you'd like to generate more traffic to your website, is that a top priority for you?"

"Yes, it is"

The second qualifying question follows on to give you an indication of what timescale your prospect is working to.

"When you say it is a priority, in an ideal world how soon did you want to have a better arrangement in place?"

At this point, you can get anything from *"Well, it's a priority but in all honestly we wouldn't look at this for at least nine months" "If we can find the right deal then we'll change quickly"*

If you get a positive answer to the first question, then you have what I'd call a qualified lead, and the only issue is to establish where in your pipeline that lead will sit.

It also gives you the option to decide what course of action you'd like to take with that lead. Sales cycles differ from one product to another but as a guide for example, if they want to fix the issue in the short to medium term (1-6 months) in other words it is genuinely a priority then you'll want to move this along to a face to face appointment at this stage.

However if the timeline is longer than that you may wish to opt for another course action. You can arrange to send them some further information on your Company, your product/service, and set up a call back at an agreed time between you to talk further. Your lead then goes into your CRM system and adds to the growing pipeline of opportunities that you'll be developing by following **Straightforward Approach™**

The third qualifying question tests whether you've gained sufficient trust, demonstrated sufficient credibility and given them enough confidence in you to take the next step:

"John, this is absolutely something we can help you with. If I can show you how we could achieve what you're looking for, would that be useful to you?"

Or

"This is definitely something we can deliver for you. We've helped many other clients who were in exactly the same situation as you, and I could show you how we did it, would that be useful to you?"

Or

"This is definitely something we can help you with. If I can show you how we'd deliver what you're looking for, would you be happy to talk it through with me?"

So there you have the three qualifiers in action. Miss anyone of them out at your peril. The temptation when you're on the phone sometimes is to "hear what you need to hear" in order to move things on, rather than hearing what is actually being said. If your prospect doesn't qualify to move to the next step in **your** process then accept that and take appropriate action. There will be more prospects out there that will qualify perfectly, so don't feel the heat to "force" things. Ask the questions, get the answers, take action accordingly-That's a **Straightforward Approach™!**

Part Three:

Securing sales appointments and dealing with objections

Chapter 7

How to set solid sales appointments

There are a number of ways to get a date in the diary once you're dealing with a qualified prospect. For example, the final version of the third qualifying question above can be used as a lead in to setting an appointment.

"This is definitely something we can help you with. If I can show you how we'd deliver what you're looking for, would you be happy to talk it through with me?"

"Yes, makes sense"

"Great, then let's get together. How's your diary looking not next week but the week after?"

(See further section: Getting a date in the diary for ideas on how to progress from here)

Here's another very powerful way to move from qualification to setting an appointment.

Making a suggestion

Once you've gained commitment from your prospect the next step in the process is to set your appointment. Without doubt the most effective outcome that you can achieve at this point is to get in front of your potential customer. You can send all the information you like by post and e mail (and there are times when in the case of a genuine request for information *before* someone will see you or as a condition of seeing you, you'll need to send it, and it is the right thing to do) but sitting opposite someone gives you the very best opportunity to win the business. So, how do you go about setting the appointment? This can be the part of the conversation where a bit of tension can creep in. The tension can be felt both ways. You may feel tense because you know you're close to setting an appointment, and from their perspective there is a good chance that at this point in other conversations they have had with salespeople they've been on the receiving end of some pretty traditional and all too familiar lines. I'm not knocking them, they can and do work.

"I'm in your area on..."

"I'm passing your door on..." "I'm seeing another Company close to you on. Why don't I come in and see you?"

"It would be great to meet with you, I can do Tuesday at 10, or Thursday at 9, which one will suit you best?"

I want to suggest to you that there's a better way to do it. I'm going to give you a line now that has helped me set thousands of sales appointments over the years. Here it is:

"Would you mind if I made a suggestion to you?"

The words need to be delivered in an almost "afterthought" kind of way, and definitely not in any kind of rigid scripted way, like some sort of Dalek.

"Would.You.Mind.If.I.Made.A.Suggestion.To.You….Would.You.Mind. If.I.Made.A
Suggestion.To.You"

Your tone and pace needs to convey the impression that this is something that you've just thought would be a great idea.

On the face of it nothing too revolutionary going on here but there is a lot of psychology at play behind the words.
If someone asks your permission to make a suggestion to you what is your normal reaction? The vast majority of people through sheer human nature will reply with *"Yes, ok, go on what is it?"* If you doubt this fact, over the next few days when you're having conversations with people in any situation simply ask at an appropriate *time "Would you mind if I made a suggestion to you?"* and see what responses you get. Apart from the human nature aspect there is another quite subtle thing going on when you ask the question like this. You are effectively giving complete control to the person you're speaking with to decide for themselves if they are happy for you to make your suggestion. This is counter to what people are used to salespeople doing. Typically salespeople like to keep complete control over their conversations and will particularly at the point they want to set an appointment be quite forceful and direct about what they are going to do. "Once you've had a positive response to your question you move forward with:

Gaining agreement to meet

Here are some alternative approaches you can use to secure an agreement to meet you.

"Well, I've been listening carefully to what you've said, and in particular when you explained that (now repeat their main issue/concern with their current provider or what they highlighted as being the most important thing to them in relation to your product or service such as an increase in or decrease in..) That's something that we've been able to solve successfully for many of our current clients. My thinking is that we could get together for half an hour so I can better understand your specific set of circumstances, and of course I'd be happy to cover any questions you may have about our work. Does that make sense?"

"Yes it does"

Or

"Well, I've been listening carefully to what you've said and in particular when you explained that... You'll be the judge of course but I'm confident it's something we can help you with, and my thinking is that we could get together for half an hour to talk through your situation. It's by no means a sales pitch! , we don't work that way I can assure you, but my hope would be that I leave you with a positive impression so that when you do look to replace/review/change/evaluate/consider....you'll have been sufficiently impressed to make sure we're part of the process-Would you be happy to meet on that basis?"

"OK"

Or (more direct option)

"Seems like we have a lot of common ground John, why don't we meet? Would you be happy to do that?"

"Of course!"

Getting a date in the diary

It's always easier for people to say yes to a meeting when the date gives them some breathing space and they don't feel like they're on the spot to see you immediately. (Unless of course they want to, and it suits your schedule too) A good way to take the heat out of this part of the process is to first help them to relax by saying:

"That's great. How does your diary look not next week but week commencing…?"

"Yes, that looks ok"

"Is there any particular day that works best for you that week?"

At this point you'll often get people talking you through their diary. *"Not the Tuesday because I'm out, Wednesdays aren't good for me, the Friday looks good"*

You now continue with:

"Friday works well for me too. Do you want to see me in the morning or a bit later in the day?"

"Morning is good"

"So, shall we say 10.00am, or does 11.00am work better for you?"

"10 am is fine"

"Excellent, and I'm coming along to 123 The Street London EC1 1AB is that's right?"

"Yes"

"And just so I know John, am I ok for parking there?"

"Yes, plenty of parking on site here"

So at this point you have an appointment in your diary with a qualified prospect. You will have seen that in setting your meeting you've asked your prospect to give some thought to it, to be involved in the process, making decisions on the best day and time to see you. You've also gone against traditional sales thinking which dictates that you have to force a day/time on the prospect. You've allowed the prospect to take the lead here in identifying a day/time that works best for them. You have not tried to overtly control the situation although again there are some subtle psychological forces at play in you giving up or seemingly giving up control of the appointment setting process. You are showing that you are confident and relaxed enough to allow the prospect to decide what's best for them. By suggesting that the appointment takes place the week after next, again you are allowing them some space. Interestingly many times when you do this you'll find that if they have a space for you earlier they will say so, but if you suggest the earlier date even if they have a space they'll opt to push it into the following week. It's a strange quirk of human nature. All of this deepens your relationship and acts as an even further qualification process. It's easy to force people into seeing you, but what's the point of that? You want to be seeing people who want to see you! They want to see you because it makes sense, not because you have forced the issue by manipulating an appointment. It is a futile game to force appointments that later pull out. Have confidence in the quality of the conversation you've had with the person and you'll only be setting well qualified appointments.

Now cement your appointment

"Thank you John, I've already put that in my diary but I'm going to send you an appointment confirmation via Outlook and I'd be grateful if you can just respond to that when you get it. I'm really looking forward to meeting with you and thanks for your time today"

As soon as you get off the phone send an "Appointment" by Outlook which requests a response from your prospect. Once received the appointment appears in both of your Outlook calendars.

In the subject line for the appointment confirmation use the title Short Meeting with (Your Name) from (Your Company) Again a bit of psychology at play here. As the meeting date draws nearer and if your prospects diary is becoming busy and he or she needs to free up some time they are much less likely to cancel "a short meeting" than what they may perceive as being a long one!

I also recommend confirming your appointment with a brief letter a few days beforehand. You will find that if you set your appointments using the **Straightforward Approach™** method you will have a very low cancellation rate. You can be assured that everyone you sit in front of will represent a genuine opportunity to do business.

Appointment setting – a final word
Never forget that if you don't ask for an appointment it's highly unlikely that you'll get one. I know that sounds obvious but it's really easy to have great conversations with people but miss the opportunity to get a date in the diary. Just be bold. When you sense that you're at that point of being able to suggest getting together, do it. Don't hold back or hesitate. There's nothing worse than getting off the phone and realising that you missed an opportunity.

It's not the end of the world because you will be following back up with your prospect anyway, but if you can, go for it on your first call. You really have got to be in it to win it. As Wayne Gretzky the famous Canadian ice hockey legend once said "You miss every shot that you don't take".

Chapter 8

Dealing with objections

The whole ethos behind **Straightforward Approach™** is to give you a framework that actually works in the real world. Therefore, we must of course also cover the objections that are inevitably part of the sales process. Someone once said that the only two certain things in life are death and taxes. I'd like to add one more thing, and that's that if you are involved in selling as well as having to pay tax and one day join the sales territory in the sky, you will also without doubt encounter objections! The good news is that far from being something to be worried or concerned about an objection should actually we welcomed. That's right, welcomed because as you'll see when someone raises one it doesn't actually mean for one minute that they are *not* interested in what you have to say, in fact it can often mean the opposite. Objections can be raised for a whole host of reasons and I'm going to give you the tools to get to the bottom of what's really going on. Common objections handily for salespeople also fall into standard types regardless of what you're selling. Yes, the product or service may be different but the types of objection are often the same for all of us. That said, once you start making lots of calls you'll also encounter some that you just don't see coming at all, and I'll give you some guidance on how to deal with "Random objections" too. Remember, don't take objections at face value, they may or may not be real.

Now here's an important point. Contrary to a lot of material that's been written on sales over the years, you cannot and will not overcome them all. Sometimes an objection is such that it genuinely means you're not going to do business with that person, and in the spirit of Straightforward Approach, by now you should be feeling completely ok about that and realise that in fact the knowledge that "You can't win them all" will actually allow you to take the pressure off yourself, relax and not be dragged into forcing the issue.

Types of Objections

Firstly I want to give you an idea of the types of objections that you'll be coming up against. We'll then look at some specifics and categorise them. Get used to listening to what your prospects are saying, and when you're hit with an objection see if you can allocate it into one of these categories. If you can, you'll be better equipped to deal with it.

The Defence Mechanism (Sometimes referred to as the "Knee Jerk Reaction")

Over the years people in business have developed almost a subliminal in built resistance to being sold to. This unfortunately has come about often due to that person having received some pretty poor sales calls over their career and so it's no wonder they try and head you off at the pass before you even get started. One way they can do this is by throwing an objection which they get a feeling of protection from and the objective is for it to deter you from moving forward with your call. These knee jerk reactions don't mean for one minute however that the prospect has no interest in what you have to say, but you're going to have to work hard to earn the opportunity to develop the call.

The Generic Favourites

We're all familiar with these objections. These objections have been around for as long as people have been selling products and services. If you were a fly on the wall in any sales office in the country where people are making outbound calls and you could hear both sides of the conversation you'd hear these all day long regardless of the product or service.

"I'm about to go into a meeting, today's not a good day, I'm about to leave the office, can you call me next week, next month, next year, we don't have any budget for anything right now, I'll need to discuss this with others, you're too expensive, can you send me something, send me an e mail and if I'm interested I'll get back to you."

The Challenge/Confrontation

The challenge can be a little unnerving. It often comes out in the form of an ultimatum.

"Unless you can show me this, this and this, or do that, that and that, or prove this, that or the other, or give us an x% discount, or improve this or that aspect of your service we won't be doing business with you"

The presumption on the part of the person issuing the challenge is that you as the salesperson are going to cave in to whatever the demand is and start to bend over backwards to accommodate their request and in doing so win the business. I'm all for accepting reasonable challenges but you'll find with the type of person that is prone to issuing these kind of ultimatums that they unfortunately can be far from reasonable and actually quite confrontational. Fear not, I will show you how to deal with this and take the wind out of their sails.

The Hidden

Hidden objections are often cloaked in a question. For example a question such as
"Do you have any experience in our sector?" may be hiding the objection *"I'm not convinced yet that I have enough confidence that you'll be effective in our sector"* *"Do you have any flexibility on the price?"* is potentially another way of saying *"I think you're too expensive"* Again you won't really know unless you probe the reason for the question which we'll look at in objection handling techniques.

The Real

As it says on the tin, the real objection is the ultimate reason as to why your prospect is unsure of moving forward with you. Uncover what this is and successfully deal with it and you're on your way to a sale. Sometimes people will make it easy for you. They'll say things like *"I'm happy with everything you've said except for this one thing"* They'll then tell you what it is-you know where you stand.

The Condition

Not every sale is blocked due to an objection. Conditions are genuine reasons or sets of circumstances that dictate a sale at this point in proceedings is impossible. It's pointless as a salesperson to try to push forward when you're dealing with a condition. Examples of conditions could be, a signatory who needs to authorise some work is out of the office for a week, or the purchase of your product/service is dependent on another set of circumstances being in place. For example, an office fit out Company may get to a point where they are the preferred supplier but until their customer secures new premises the finer details of the work cannot be finalised.

All is not lost however when you come up against a condition. I'm going to give you a technique you can use to make things as water tight as they can be without actually writing the order.

Objection Handling Techniques

In large corporate organisations they have the luxury of being able to lock their sales teams away for weeks on end turning them into very well oiled objection handling machines-I know they do that because I've been on all those courses too! Literally days are spent on looking at different ways to deal with objections from every angle. We don't have time for that in this book so I'm going to give you some structures to work with that will cover most situations you'll encounter. In the same way that I advocate not having a script when you make your calls, I also don't advocate having set in stone responses to objections. It's about being natural. So have a read of the techniques below and play around with them on your calls. You need to develop your own style with all this so that the language you use is yours, not mine.

Respond don't react:

Particularly when you're new to the world of telephone prospecting it's easy to feel flustered on the phone when people put you on the spot. I can't emphasise enough the importance of staying calm, relaxed and in control of your natural tendencies to meet "fire with fire" If people are aggressive with you, remember that you are in charge here, and you'll decide whether or not you want the call to go any further. Remember, it's about working with the willing and you definitely do not need to waste your time on the phone with people who like to throw their weight around and show you and everyone else just how important they are. If you ever get a gut feeling on a call that you're really trying to open a closed door, do yourself a favour and professionally bring the call to a close-you'll lose nothing, and gain a lot of confidence from the fact that you're in charge of your own destiny. Believe me, there are thousands and thousands of people out there who will be more than happy to discuss what you have to offer. Your job through your calls is to identify who they are as quickly as possible and don't worry about those that are burning your energy.

The sponge-soak it up

I can give you a really good mental picture to have in your mind for those occasions on the phone when people are being a bit challenging, a sponge. In the same way a sponge soaks up more and more water, your job is to soak up the aggressive or difficult first responses you may get. Just think sponge. If someone wants to go on the attack about your call, let them, soak it up and just when they expect you to do what salespeople do which is to start justifying the call and selling the benefits of their product or service, I want you to do the opposite. Politely step back and explain that you think it's a good idea to draw a line under the call and leave it there. It's funny, I've had it many times when someone has started off all guns blazing and then when you make them realise that actually you're ok about not having the conversation, all of a sudden they want it more than you do!

Ignore it and ask a question

It's natural to want to answer every objection as it comes up. However, sometimes the best thing you can do is ignore it completely and see whether it resurfaces later on. For example someone may say to you early on in the conversation *"I knew someone who bought your product and they didn't like it"* Now, you could get really bogged down in finding out who the person was, why they didn't like it and then start to counter with all sorts of features, advantages and benefits of your product/service. The point is in this case, so what if someone else bought it and didn't like it? What relevance does that have to your prospect? So, instead you can just say *"Oh, that's interesting"* and then ask them a question to get the focus of the conversation back on them. If the objection is a major issue rest assured you'll be hit with it again later on in the conversation in which case you can deal with it then. Don't "bite" on every opportunity to deal with an objection. In my experience many objections will simply disappear if you don't give them any importance, but if you let them de rail you, you can end up having conversations that you don't need to have and which ultimately just end up taking you away from your goal of your call.

Side step and ask a question

The side step is a really great technique. It buys you some time and puts you in charge in terms of when you choose to deal with the issue being raised. Let's say you are talking about your product/service and are very much in the fact finding part of the conversation and your prospect says *"I'm not sure we'd get the return on investment we'd need from this"* Again you will be tempted to answer the objection there and then. However, it's better to answer it when you have the full facts about your prospects situation once you've uncovered the ammunition that is going to help you demonstrate your value. The way to do this is *"Of course return on investment is essential. Thank you for raising that now, I'm going to cover that for you shortly but can I just ask"* Then ask a question. Later on in your conversation you may find that you don't need to cover the ROI issue in order to set your appointment. After all it's far better if you can to deal with it face to face. However, if from your prospects point of view they need it answering before they agree to an appointment then of course you'll need to cover it. The key point here again is don't answer or deal with things straight away that you don't need to.

Feel Felt Found

A favourite of mine. It works in any and every situation, and again buys you some thinking time. Feel Felt Found has been a life saver for generations of salespeople and is particularly helpful to people new to sales who may initially lack confidence when facing objections. I'd suggest that having **Feel Felt Found** in your tool box should give you massive confidence that you can deal with all and any objections-now how good is that!

The idea here is that whatever the objection you're going to put yourself in that persons shoes and show them that you validate their concern. People want to be heard and too many sales people jump in with a "*Yes but*" before their prospect has even finished voicing their concerns. So let's take the objection "*Your minimum order value is too high*" You start with "*I can understand how you feel*" The next part of the technique enables you to show even more empathy by stating that other people you've dealt with have been in the same situation, and this again adds more validity to their point of view So, you continue with "*Many of our current customers **felt** exactly the same way when we first started talking to them about our service*" Now you're going to answer the objection but importantly the answer is not going to be coming from you directly but rather you're going to get your customers to answer your objection for you! The technique finished therefore with "*What they **found** however, is that although our order limits were at first glance a little higher than they were looking for, the cost savings they made added to the excellent customer service they received made it more than worth their while to change suppliers*"

Feel-Put yourself in their shoes

Felt- Further validation of their concern showing that others saw things the same way

Found- Now answer the objection but using the experience of you current customers.

Confront it

As much of a fan as I am of avoiding conflict at all costs during the sales process sometimes you get eliminate an objection by simply confronting it. The voice tone you use here needs to be spot on otherwise you'll come across as being too combative. The way this works is that you put the onus on the other person almost to prove their point. Particularly useful when you know for sure that what they've said is incorrect. If they do prove it then of course you'll do your level best to answer their concern but this one has a funny way of making people see for themselves that their objection is flawed Take the objection *"Your cars fuel economy is too high versus the XYZ model"* (incorrect) *"That's interesting, what are you basing that on?" "Well, I read it in a magazine somewhere" "Ok, which one was that? I haven't seen the article" "I'm not sure it was one of the motoring ones, I'm definitely right on it though" "I see, I need to read that article thanks for bringing it up because the stats I have are that our car is actually 5 MPG better than the XYZ, so we need to go back and double check our figures"* Once you've countered the objection like this move on quickly by asking a question. The idea is not to get into a back and forth about fuel economy but simply to show that you know your onions so to speak.

Question/re state/isolate/answer

It's very effective to get your prospect to be more specific about their objection. It makes sure that you have fully understood what they've said, and also makes them put some thought into what they're saying. It shows them that you are not someone who will just take things at face value. Take the objection *"I can't make an appointment at the moment there's just too much going on"* Firstly you need to question it. "*I understand how busy you are; when you said busy at the moment what did you mean?*" "*Well over the next week its manic here, we've got all sorts of contractors coming in*" You now need to re state the objection to show that you understand what's going on in their mind. You do this by using "*So what you're saying is..* " In this case, "*So what you're saying is that due to the work that taking place this week, the last thing you want to do is add to your diary is that right?*" "*Spot on*" Now isolate the objection, in other words make sure there's nothing else that would prevent them from setting an appointment with you. "*In addition to that is there any other reason why you wouldn't want to meet?*" "*No, it's just the time this week*" You're now at a point where you can answer the objection and in this case as clearly your prospect is under a bit of pressure I'd suggest you ease that pressure by not just putting things off for a week but until the week after next. "*I understand, I should have been clearer, I didn't mean that we meet this week or even next, I was looking at week commencing the...*"

Ask them what would put their mind at rest about their objection

This is another great one for getting your prospect to join in, get thinking and actually solve their own objection. The way it works is like everything we do, very straightforward. Take the example "*I don't know your Company, never heard of you so not sure I want to meet at this stage*" What's really going on here is that your prospect is doubting your credibility in some way. Just ask them. "*I understand, what would put your mind at rest on that?*" So much more powerful than diving straight in with a pitch again about how great you are. Ask the question and let them answer. "*Well, if I was able to speak with some people in this area that you've worked with, that would help*" "*I see, no problem, so if we can arrange for you to speak personally with 3 of our clients you'd be happy to see us would you?*" "*Well yes*" "*Ok, here are the names and numbers of three people who'll be more than happy to speak about how happy they've been with our service-Let's get a date in the diary for us to meet and in the meantime that gives you some time to speak with our clients and you can tell me what they said when I see you"*

Confirm that objections have been dealt with

Always check that the objection has been satisfactorily dealt with. If you try to move on when it hasn't you'll hit problems, so just ask. Use questions like:

"Have I answered that for you?"
"Are you happy with that now?"
"Does that make sense now?"
"Does that answer that one for you, or would you like some further clarification"
"Have covered that for you? If not, please let me know."

I'm now going to cover the most likely objections you'll encounter in the order that you'll encounter them whilst working within the **Straightforward Approach™** framework. In each case I'll categorise the objection in terms of type and give you a couple of alternative ways to respond, different in their style and approach, and the fun for you is to use them all and work out which ones work best for you. I've said time and again, this is a book that you need to take action on so dive in and get objection handling.

I dealt with the main objections you'll come up against at reception level earlier on, so for the purposes of this section we'll start with:

Pre empt the objection

This is a great technique. You already know every single regular objection that you will encounter when you're on the phone promoting you product or service. The power in that is that you are able to practice, practice and practice some more all of the different ways to answer these objections. You really should never be in a position where you're caught off guard so to speak. Knowing what your objections are likely to be before you even pick your phone up also enables you to use the pre-empting method of dealing with an objection. Let's say for example that you are a new start up but you yourself have had years of experience in the industry. The objection that could be raised is *"You've only been in business for 6 months, we tend to work with more established businesses"* Knowing this early on in your conversation with your prospect you can find a way to say without prompting by them: *"Although the business was only established 6 months ago, what our current customers are finding is that because I and my partner have over 30 years combined experience in the industry they feel like they're working with a really long established Company because of our knowledge and the way we go about things"* Think about the main objections you'll face and then practice ways to pre-empt them. The knack is to drop your pre-empt into the conversation naturally. You don't need to make a big deal about it, just drop it in and believe me the subliminal message will be well and truly planted so that if the objection crosses your prospects mind they will automatically stop themselves raising it because you've already answered it!

Objections on reaching your decision maker:

Defence Mechanism Examples

Once you're through to your decision maker you'll remember that you are going to check that you are talking with the right person. At this point more often than not they will confirm that for you, but occasionally here you can come up against a couple of what on the face of it seem like fairly prickly responses. I'll outline them in a second but you need to understand that if you hit these responses it has absolutely nothing to do with you or what you've said but it can have much to do with what is going on in that person's working day when you call, what kind of mood they are in and a whole host of other aspects that you simply cannot know before you call them. These two objections fall under the defence mechanism category. The key to dealing with these is to stay calm, relaxed and focused on your objective.

Is this a sales call?

The *"Is this a sales call?"* objection is normally thrown out there either by people who to be frank don't particularly enjoy receiving sales calls, or by someone who ordinarily wouldn't mind the call but on this occasion is having a bad day, is pushed for time, under pressure, or has just put the phone down to a salesperson who has not studied the **Straightforward Approach™**. It is often delivered in a fairly aggressive manner.

How to handle

Due to the likely agitated state of the person my advice here is to withdraw tactically and offer your contact both a way out and the victory (for now!) What I mean is that you're not going to get very far talking with someone who has their hackles up before you even start. It can be possible to move the conversation from here and I've shown you how to do it, but if you don't get a "bite" best to withdraw and live to fight another day. Let's just keep it simple. Your contact is expecting you to say that no, it isn't a sales call. Their question to an extent is rhetorical. They've asked it because they actually have a high degree of certainty that it is, and may be just spoiling for a confrontation. So what you're going to do is say the opposite of what they are expecting, but then suggest yourself that the call goes no further!" The psychology (and reality) at play here is that you are not by any means over anxious to have a conversation now if it doesn't suit them. It plays on the old adage that people always want what they can't have. The thing that they aren't going to be able to have right now is a conversation with you, unless *they* really work hard at getting you to join in!

This is what it looks like:

"Yes, it is John, although I sense that this isn't a good time to speak with you and the last thing I want to do is take up your time when it's not convenient. No, problem I'm happy to call back.....Can I ask, is there a time of day that works better than others for you to discuss X "(The X of course is the major benefit that your product/service offers)

At this point you may get a response indicating that your X is definitely not of interest in which case you've lost nothing. You may be given a time of day to call back so you've had a result and now have a warmer call back. However, you may also be asked a second question along the lines of *"Well quickly, what is it you wanted to talk about?"* Never, ever feel pressured or rushed to engage in a conversation that you don't want to have, and believe me, if they are pushed for time you don't want to be having this one. So continue with..

"As I said it's regarding X but it wouldn't be right for me to just rattle off some benefits of what we do without knowing more about your situation, is there a day/time I can call back so we can both discuss this together?"

Your prospect will either give you a day and time, or if what you have to talk about genuinely wasn't of interest they won't, instead electing to say something like *"You'll just have to call back"* in which case I'd suggest you move on and don't worry about calling back.

How did you get my name?
Again, this one is another fairy defensive response and so as with the objection above my advice here is to answer their question in a straightforward way, but at the same time let them know that you're completely ok with the call ending now if that's what they want.

How to handle

The key here is to be up front. If you were told their name by a colleague then say *so "I called yesterday and asked who would be responsible for X, and was told that's you John, apologies if I have that wrong, should I be speaking with someone else?"* The ball is back with them now so wait for their response and take it from there.

If you have a name on a list that you've purchased, then say *"Our research team have provided me with your details John, they spend a lot of time identifying companies who based on what they do may be a good fit for our services"*

We've discussed the merits of finding people via the business portal Linkedin, so don't be shy in saying something along the lines of *"I like to do my own research before I contact a Company John, and it was whilst carrying that out that I read that you head up ABC there, apologies if I have that wrong, is there someone else I should be speaking with about...?"*

I don't have time to talk about this now

I touched on this one earlier on when looking at why it's important to ask people if it's a convenient time to talk. In addition to the advice in that section here's a bit more to help you with this particular objection.

There are usually two different situations at play here and unless you know which one you're dealing with you can be in danger of entering the longest telephone tennis match in history. If you assume for instance that you're being told that this isn't a good time to talk because it genuinely isn't then your natural response is likely to be *"No problem, I'll call back"* Problem is that if this isn't a genuine statement, when you call back, and if you get through, again I can guarantee you that it will be another episode of *"It's not a good time to talk"*

How to handle

"That's not a problem at all John. Can I just check, I'm happy to call back, but to save us both time, I won't do so unless X (your major benefit) is of interest. What would you prefer I do?"

They have to make decision now and be straight with you either way. Ask your question and then be quiet. Let them decide where this call goes. This response goes against what you'll read in most sales books, manuals and what is taught on many sales training courses where the emphasis is on simply gaining agreement that you'll be calling back. Gaining agreement to call back like this on an unidentified day and time is frankly pointless. You'll be playing the chasing game which is a burn of your energy and more importantly time. Slightly better is gaining agreement to call back on a specific day, and better still an agreed time. However as I say neither of these address the real issue, the "elephant in the room" which is do they genuinely want you to call back? The **Straightforward Approach™** method gives them the opportunity to tell you the truth either way. It saves you and them time and will reduce stress on both sides of the call.

Generic Favourites

We're happy with who we're with

When you think about it unless you're selling something that is literally unique or innovative (which you may be in which case you can be up against some objections that I'll cover later) the person you're going to speak with is always going to have "a supplier" in place. This is because they are contractual arrangements to deliver regular daily, weekly, monthly and yearly services that the Company needs to function or the it can be that in the case of more ad hoc, one off purchases perhaps for capital equipment for example they have a preferred supplier. Either way, when you're hit with this objection it shouldn't come as surprise to you. Remember what I said, after a while you will know every single objection that you're likely to encounter so once you've got really polished at your responses there really isn't anything at all to worry about. It's a bit like knowing what the numbers to the lottery are going to be before you even see the draw!.

How to handle

Traditional sales responses to this one unfortunately centre on the idea that it's best to make the person see the error of their ways by outlining that their product/service is better. The word *"but"* is a killer to sales success. Do not use it. If you hear yourself saying *"Yes, but"* when answering a prospects objections stop it please. The conversation usually sounds something like *"We're using XYZ Company and I've got to say we're really happy with them"* *"Yes, but the thing is we can ...."* Game over. By saying to someone *"Yes, but"* it's almost like dismissing what they're saying and intimating that they made a poor purchasing decision in the past. Now how would you feel if someone told you that you'd made a bad purchasing decision? Exactly. A far better way to answer this one is: *"That's fine John, I never thought for one minute that you would not have a current supplier, and I'm sure that they're doing a great job. I'm not looking to rock that boat at all, but just understand better what might lead you to consider other suppliers?"*

At this point what you're looking for is the person to say that for example if they were let down on service, or costs started to creep up that they may look elsewhere. This opens up an opportunity for you to continue with:

"That's interesting, I understand why you feel like that, many of the companies that we're currently helping felt exactly the same way when we first spoke with them. What they found was that it was useful for us to provide some ideas on how we would handle their contract, so that if and when the time came to consider change at least they had an option available to them-is that something you'd be happy for us to do for you?"

The key point with this one is never to infer that their current supplier is doing anything other than a great job. Your prospect is expecting you to be critical of the competition, so do the opposite and you'll be amazed at how much easier the conversation becomes.

We don't have any budget

You can't sell anything to people that can't pay for it, but you need to establish if this is a real objection or not.

How to handle

Firstly you could ignore it. *"We have no budget"* Respond with *"I understand, can I ask.."* Now ask a question. If the objection comes back you can question it a bit more *"As I said, we have no budget" "That's ok, can I ask, when you say there's no budget can you help me understand that a bit more, did you mean there's no budget this quarter, this month?" "No budget until our financial year starts in June" "Oh, I see, so what you're saying is that until the new financial year starts you're not really in a position to talk about this, is that right?" "Yes" "I see, in addition to that though is there any other reason you wouldn't want to look at this?" "No, it's just the budget" "Not a problem, I didn't think for a minute that you'd have budget available for this tight now, in fact my call was really just to better understand how you.."* Now just get back into a conversation. Sure, if the budget objection is real then this may be a lead for your pipeline as opposed to an appointment for the diary.

Can you send me something?

People ask to be "sent something" for two main reasons. Firstly they genuinely want to evaluate your Company and what's on offer. Secondly, they are simply not interested one iota in what you have to offer but are too polite to say so. Like I've said before it would be so much better if people were just straight with each other, it would save such a lot of time. Instead, they choose to ask for you to get some further information over to them. Problem is that many sales people then get involved in the chasing game. They falsely perceive the request for information to be interest on the part of the prospect and begin pursuing the sale, the sale that is not there in the first place. The key here is to stop this pointless merry go round right at the start of proceedings.

How to handle

"I'd be really happy to send you something, but can I just check something with you first?"

"Yes, what is it?"

"Well I'm sure you're busy so I don't want to add to your in box unnecessarily. Often when people say send me something it's because they're genuinely interested in X – (the X is your major benefit) but equally sometimes they say it because they actually have no interest in X (get your benefit in again) and want to end the call. Guided by you, but what in particular did you want information on, or would you prefer we leave things here?"

Alternative

"I'd be really happy to send you something, but I want to make it relevant to your situation. What aspect of X (again the X is your major benefit statement) did you want information on?"

If your prospect can't give you a sensible answer then that's a good sign they just want to end the call. There's something very empowering about being in control of who you want and don't want to send things to.

If you do decide to e mail some information or send something hard copy in the mail, before you end the call make arrangements on when you'll be speaking again with your prospect. A good way to do this is to say *"Great I'll get that over to you, but before you go I'm sure you dislike telephone tennis as much as I do. Can we arrange now a good day/time for us to speak again-it will save us both a lot of time"*

If you get any kind of evasive answer on this one then take a view on whether this is a prospect worth your time writing an e mail or letter and the cost of a stamp.

Can you call me next month, next week, next year?

Similar to the *"Can you send me something?"* People will ask you to call them next week, next month, or next year for one of two reasons. You probably know where I'm going with this one! It's either because they genuinely want to talk with you again, or they don't and are too polite to say.

How to handle

"Of course, I'd be delighted to call you back, but can I just check something with you first?" "Yes, what is it?" Well I'm sure you're busy so I don't want to take up your time unnecessarily. Often when people ask me to call back its because they have a genuine interest in X (your major benefit) but sometimes it's because actually they have no interest in X and want to end the call. Guided by you, do you want to schedule a call back or would you prefer we leave things here?"

Now, if your prospect says that yes they do genuinely want you to call back, don't leave it open ended, arrange a good day and time, or date (if a longer term calk back) to call.

Need to discuss with others before I agree to see you

If someone tells you that they need to discuss things with others before they agree to meet with you, then you need to re evaluate whether you are actually speaking with the right person in the first place. You need to tread carefully though as no one likes to feel like second best. Confronting this one is a way to get to the bottom of things.

How to handle

"I understand, can I ask though what particular aspect of what we've discussed will you be speaking with your colleague about?" Other questions you can ask are: *"That's understandable, a lot of people I deal with work that way, can I ask though, will you be recommending that we meet?"* or *"That's understandable, a lot of people I deal with work that way but can I ask, if it were your decision alone, would you be recommending that we meet?"* The previous question will give you a feel for how positive about you/your product your contact is. Any kind of vague answer at this point usually indicates that their initial response was simply designed to let you down gently. Also go with, *"That's understandable, a lot of people I deal with work that way. Can I ask though, what is the specific process at your Company for deciding on new suppliers?"* What you're looking to do here is get a better understanding of the buying process and in doing so you'll get a good feel for how much influence the person you're speaking with has. In some cases you will need to meet first with an influencer before perhaps a second meeting with the influencer and the ultimate decision maker together. If however you sense from your questions that the person you're dealing with simply doesn't have any authority despite what you may have been led to believe, you need to work the call around so that you can speak with the more senior contact direct. A good way to do this is *"Thanks for explaining that to me, can I make a suggestion? " "Yes" " Well I've listened to the process that you have here and by the sounds of it I'd be saving you a fair bit of time if I were to speak with X directly. Is that something we can arrange together? For example I can set up a conference call where all three of us can speak, or should I*

just call them personally?" You need to give them the option of being included in the process but often you'll find that they are happy to have had the issue moved on from them and they'll give you the go ahead to make the call to their colleague. Sometimes, if your contact is a genuine influencer who needs to be involved in the process, and they've liked what you've had to say, they will take the lead and arrange a call. It's about showing them that you're not trying to go over their head in any way, but actually that it's a team game.

The Challenge

I'll give you one minute

Some people like to put you on the spot. They will say things like *"Look, you've got one minute to convince me of.."* It's a challenge they are laying down. The sub text is *"I'll give you a minute, you show me how great you are selling and how great your product or service is and then I'll decide what happens next"* Sales people down the years have been drawn into this one time and time again. It is a slippery slope believe me. If you give in to temptation and start pitching, in my opinion you have lost all credibility and have no chance of influencing where that conversation goes. You can end up giving war and peace on your product or services benefits only for your prospect to turn round and say *"Sorry you've not convinced me"* or even worse *"Sorry, you've run out of time"* Certain personality types are prone to laying down "The challenge". They're often what some people refer to as Type A personalities, I call them "doers" Always in a hurry, don't want the small talk just the nitty gritty.

How to handle

You can have a lot of fun with this one. The key is to completely relax and not be flustered one iota by your demanding questioner.

You need to do two things. One is slow them down, and two let them know that you're not the kind of salesperson that performs like a seal at the zoo! Obviously we won't use those words. We'll be far more subtle than that. OK, so first of all, slow them down. In a sense this contradicts some of what I've said earlier in the book about voice matching, but in this case you're going to slow them down because they've issued the challenge. If you were already into a sensible conversation with them I'd advocate voice matching them as this style of person reacts well to that. To slow them down, you need to keep your pace relaxed and steady and say *"I appreciate that you just want the bullet points but we're not the sort of Company to pitch what we do. We prefer to have a conversation to listen and learn more about your situation rather than talking about us, and that kind of conversation can't be had in a minute. If you're genuinely open to finding out if we have some common ground I'll call you back at a better time-What would you suggest we do?"* Your prospect won't be used to this. Surely as a salesperson you're meant to be like a pitching and closing machine aren't you? Call them back? What would you suggest?-Not what they're used to at all.

Now they may insist that you've got one minute, and if they do I strongly suggest that you stick rigidly to your position and just thank them for their time and say again that the conversation wouldn't be done justice in a minute so if they are not happy to re schedule a better time to talk, no problem, you'll leave it there. The secret is to then do exactly that-leave it there, remove from your call list and remind yourself of the importance of working with the willing.

You will know yourself that often the things we want most are those we can't have, or don't think we can have and this approach taps into that part of human nature. When I was selling direct marketing services many years ago we used to use a two call system to sell to Senior Marketing Directors. The process was a call on day one to qualify and outline the service and then a very tight re qualification at the end of the call to set up and agreed call back the next day. On the call back the conversation was very straightforward. They either decided that yes they were going ahead or no they weren't. Any other answer like wanting to think about it, confer with others, not had a chance to look at it etc was dealt with by simply suggesting to the prospect that we left it there, we had other people to call so best to take it as they were not going forward, the project was closing that day so no problem. Interestingly a good number of people who originally said they couldn't make a decision all of a sudden now wanted in. The reason is clear. They had been told that they couldn't do it. Now, the example I've just given I stress relates to telesales which is a different discipline entirely but the psychology still applies, take something away and people want it all the more.

What are you selling?

This is another quite aggressive response. People who say this to you tend to have a very strong in built resistance to salespeople often due to some very bad experiences in the past. This challenge assumes that you *are* selling. The concept of people actually calling to establish whether or not what they have is of potential benefit is an alien one to many in business. Moreover, the concept that the person calling will be very much guided by the person being called as to what happens next is even more off the chart! If you've called, you must be selling, right? Well we know the answer to that is actually, no, we're calling to find out if we have any common ground and we can't possibly know whether we'll be selling our product or service at this stage, to a large degree it's out of our control because the sale or possible sale will happen because it makes sense to the person we're calling, not by us because we've pushed it.

How to handle

As with the challenge in the previous example, I can't emphasise enough the need to stay calm, relaxed and unflustered. You've got absolutely nothing to be concerned about here. I stress again we're looking to work with the willing, not force the unwilling to work with us. Have a go with these responses, but if it's not sounding like your prospect is coming around at all, no problem, politely and respectfully withdraw, there are plenty of other people for you to talk with.

"I'll be frank with you, I have no idea whatsoever at this stage even whether what we do is of potential benefit to you, so the last thing I'm going to do is assume that it is and start selling, it's just not the way we do things here, I don't like it when people do it to me so I certainly don't do it to others" In response to this you may get something like *"Well what is it that you do?"* This at least gives you an opportunity to start a conversation.

"I'm sorry if I gave you that impression, I have no idea at this stage if.."

"Apologies, what gave you that impression?" This is a good one because the prospect will often start to talk about what they don't like about sales calls etc. You then of course completely agree with them like this:

"I'm sorry what gave you that impression?" *"Well, every call I get is a sales call, people being pushy and not listening to no for an answer, it really gets on my nerves"* *"That makes two of us then I get those calls too and they just really get up my nose. I don't like it, and I certainly don't work that way myself. At this stage I have no idea whatsoever even whether what we do is of potential benefit to you, so the last thing I'm going to do is assume that it is and start selling, it's just not the way we do things here"* Then continue with *"Are you ok to talk for a moment?"* You will be able to tell from the persons tone whether they are softening a bit in their stance. If they're not I recommend that you leave it there.

"I appreciate that you don't want to take sales calls and it's not a problem at all, can I suggest we leave this here" I always find it interesting that when you make someone realise that you're different in your approach, a straightforward approach, they will if they've been a bit aggressive or on occasions even rude, start to apologise for their tone, saying that they appreciate you're doing your job etc and it isn't personal. Some will even go a step further, I've had people saying things like *"Really sorry I spoke with you like that, it's not for us but I do know a business associate who may have a need for your services, here's his details!"* Yes, it does happen like that sometimes!

The Condition

A condition is different to an objection in that it's not so much an opinion as to why a prospect can't agree to an appointment for example, or to give you a decision on something but it's a reason based on facts. An example is your prospect wants to meet with you but does all their meetings with their co manager in the department and so simply can't see you on your own. The co manager is away on holiday for 2 weeks. To try to overcome this is not the way to go. It's a condition and there's nothing you can do about it so don't force the issue. Another example is a prospect says that due to budget restrictions they have been advised to cancel all appointments with potential suppliers until after the next quarter has ended. Again, you will not win any friends by pushing it at this stage. Practice recognising conditions versus objections. Nothing annoys prospects more than them being open about a condition and then a sales person treating it like an objection. When faced with a condition simply ask your prospects what they'd like you to do and take your lead from them. They'll appreciate your professionalism.

Wild card objections/comments

Once you've been making outbound phone calls for a while you'll inevitably come up against what I call the wild card objection. By its very nature it's not one you can really plan for, you just have to think on your feet when they come up. An example may be that the person you're speaking with tells you that the firm they're working for don't know it yet but they're about to leave and so they won't be in a position to see you or progress anything about your product/service. If people sense that you're a warm open person they'll at times reveal quite personal information about themselves or others. My only advice is to avoid giving any kind of personal opinion about their situation. Empathise with what they're saying but be very non committal on anything personal. Always assume that your calls are being recorded. Keep it professional and bring the call to a close.

You're in charge

I spoke earlier in the book about working with the willing. Remember, you're in charge here. You can decide to speak with who you want to. If someone is giving you a really hard time, being rude, or just being overly difficult trying to show how clever they are you don't have to put up with it. Politely, respectfully and professionally bring the conversation to an end and move on. Ironically, those people who are prone to being the most difficult on the phone can be those who secretly would like to be able to do what you're doing. Namely, having the confidence to pick the phone up and call someone they don't know. Never let anything anyone says to you on a phone call get to you or affect your positive attitude to what you're doing. You are building your business, you are investing your time in your future. You are going places and are taking action. I take my hat off to you. Winning in business is about taking action, action, and more action. So, ignore anyone who gives you a hard time. Dale Carnegie explains in his brilliant timeless huge best seller How To Win Friends and Influence People that there is nothing to gain by telling people that they're wrong, it gets you nowhere fast. However tempted you may be (and you will be) to take someone on don't ever do it, it's a pointless activity. Yes you could in many cases win the battle but you'll definitely lose the war. Over the years I've had some utterly ridiculous things said to me by people on the phone where it would have been so easy to systematically de construct their argument. When I was younger and less wise to the ways of the World I did just that, took people on, won the argument and put the phone down with a feeling of satisfaction. It didn't however change the fact that on that particular call I hadn't set an appointment, made a sale, or whatever my desired outcome had been. So, in the face of hostility, take a massive deep breath, relax and move on.

Follow Up

These are the two most powerful words in sales and business development. It makes sense that now you have worked hard to make your calls, develop relationships and opportunities for you to maximise those opportunities by following up with people. I'm not talking about being a nuisance. I'm talking about getting back to people within a sensible timeframe to hear their feedback on what you initially discussed. As much as some sales training would have us believe, it isn't always the case that you're able to move forward with a prospect on the first call, or the second, or even the third. People will make decisions within different time frames, and if you've kept your part of the bargain by keeping in touch when they asked, guess what? Yes, when it comes to the time they're willing and able to move forward you'll be in pole position. I'm not talking here about chasing shadows. If you follow the advice in this book you will already know how to separate those prospects worth working with (work with the willing) and those where frankly you'll be chasing shadows if you keep getting back to them. I'm talking about following up with people where based on the conversation (s) you've had it makes sense to keep things alive. There is more and more comment out there that we live in a multi touch marketing world where prospects will require multiple "touches" from your Company before they'll buy from you. A touch can be a look at your website, and e mail, a call, another call, maybe a letter. Multi touch makes sense, so why is it then that so many people fail to follow up in the sales process. The answer is that a lot of sales people have been conditioned to expect everything to happen right now. Further, the people that manage them expect them to make things happen right now. So when a prospect says something like *"I can see how what you do could help us but we won't be ready to meet for 3 months"* it seems like a long , long way off and interest in that prospect falls away rather rapidly. Millions of pounds worth of business is being left on the table by people not following up as they should. Make sure you're not one of them. Use a good CRM system to keep on top of when you're due to get back to people so no opportunities slip through your net. So how many times should you follow up with someone? Difficult one this as there will always be examples of deals that have been done after long periods of time but that said here's a rule that will make life a bit easier for you. 2 short, 1 medium, 1 long. What I mean by that is if you've spoken to a prospect and based on what's been said you deem it to be a good opportunity, allow up to 2 short term follow ups within say a month. On the second follow up if your prospect is still saying yes but not now and you're happy that their intentions are genuine then go with *"I appreciate that you're not able to move forward at the moment. Can I make a suggestion, as I've called back twice now, as much as we'd love to work with you, I'll be guided by you in terms of when you think will be a good time for us to speak again within the next couple of months-what are your thoughts on that?"* In other words get them to give you the next follow up timeframe which by now falls in to our medium range 1-3 months. Whatever time frame they suggest, make a note and make your call back as suggested. If on that call you're still not making progress you have 2 options. You can either go with *"No problem, can I suggest that we leave this now until X (Pick a month that is about 6 months forward) Of course if you need us in the meantime you know where we are"* Alternatively, to keep you sane and to avoid clogging up your CRM with call backs that have little chance of converting to the next step, if you feel that you've taken things as far as you can and what initially looked like a good prospect is now looking a different story entirely the best thing you can do is bring things to a close with *"I appreciate that you're not in a position to move forward on this. Can I suggest that because we've spoke about this a few times now, that we leave it here and draw a line under it. Of course, should things change and you want to re visit it I'd be really happy to talk with you"* Mentally, you need to decide what your cut off point with a prospect is otherwise you can get involved in chasing shadows that have little prospect of moving forward. There's no hard and fast rule for how many times to follow up but you do need to have a policy and stick to it. You will know in your own mind what you're dealing with and if it looks sensible to call back 2 short, 1 medium, 1 long then do so, but equally if your gut feeling is that you're chasing your tail bring it to a close and move on. The above advice I stress relates to telemarketing not telesales where the follow up policy often needs to be a lot tighter. In telesales the modus operandi is commonly to "pitch" someone and close there and then or having pitched the opportunity to agree a call back day/time to get a decision. I mentioned earlier my own experience of pitching direct marketing services over the phone where if on the second call I got anything other than a yes or a no I would bring things to a close. There was no room for I'll think about it, call me tomorrow etc it was a completely different type of environment, a direct sales environment where the multi touch philosophy just was not applicable. Another example of direct sales environments where the much more rigid policy of follow up is in place would be advertising companies where teams of direct sales people are pitching and closing ad space. I've worked in those environments too in the West End of London where we'd be on daily sales revenue targets, so again a completely different animal to the relationship developing nature of telemarketing.

A final word on follow up. You must be strict and disciplined. Do not deceive yourself about what you have in your sales pipeline. Anyone can say *"Yeah, I've got 250 live prospects in my pipeline right now"* but if in reality the majority are "shadows" you are just kidding yourself. No one should make it into your CRM as a follow up call unless you are as sure as you can be that there is something tangible there, a decent opportunity that for reasonable reasons is taking a while to come to fruition. Before you put a prospect in your CRM ask yourself a question. Am I adding something of value here, or kidding myself? Only you will know the answer, no one will be looking, be straight and honest with yourself. If you stick to what I've told you here you'll find that some of your very best customers will come as a result of adhering to a good follow up policy. As I write this I'm thinking about a prospect I went to see last week who I initially spoke with a year ago. I had followed up as per my 2 short, 1 medium, and 1 long model and the result was a very nice contract for a range of our services. No magic in that, just common sense, follow up and you'll win business that others leave on the table.

Chapter 9

Your action plan

I can't stress enough to you just how important it is to take action, action and more action. I'm sure that by now you are feeling pretty fired up about making your calls with a high level of confidence. You now need to put it all together into your own action plan, that will keep you on track and accountable as the days, weeks and months unfold. It's natural to have a high degree of motivation when you first gain a new skill and there's the buzz of putting what you've learnt into practice. However, the people that really benefit from learning new skills are those that are able to systematically implement the skills into a daily action plan so that positive habits are formed. Opinions vary but on average for a new habit to form you need to do something 21-30 times so the first month or so will be vital to your success.

I spoke earlier in the book about the hour a day philosophy, it really is very, very powerful. Of course, if you are able to schedule more than an hour a day to make calls then go for it, I'm not going to stop you!

For the purposes of creating an action plan for you however we're using what I call the **60 Minute Power Plan.** Follow the 15 steps below and you'll be on your way to transforming your sales figures.

The 60 Minute Power Plan:

1. Block off on your Outlook Calendar (or in your paper diary) a recurring 60 minute time slot for every single day of the week Monday to Friday, plan the slots for 12 months ahead.

2. Protect this time as if it were an appointment with your biggest client. If using Outlook, colour code the time slot with a colour that you associate with success. This will be different for each person but whatever your colour is select it.

3. At the allocated time each day open up your online stopwatch ready to hit start.

4. Open up your spreadsheet of contacts or your CRM system.

5. As soon as the list is open (and I mean immediately without delay) start your online stopwatch and start dialing the first number on the list.

6. Be focused. Work consistently for 60 minutes dialing numbers, having conversations, setting appointments, generating leads.

7. After each call, make sure you update your call notes and deal with any resulting action, so if you have to send a short e mail, send it.

8. During each session make a note on a sheet of paper how many calls you've made, how many conversations you've

had with decision makers, how many appointments you've set or leads generated.

9. At the end of each session transfer your call session stats to a basic spreadsheet with relevant headings so that you can track and measure your progress

10. Make sure that you have a system that works for you for recording details of all appointments and leads generated so that you can track outcomes, and importantly keep on top of follow ups. This may be your CRM, or alternatively create a separate spreadsheet.

11. Place a white board on the wall of your office with a green figure that represents how many 60 minute slots are available in that work month. As you complete each session place next to the green figure in blue the number of sessions you've completed that month. The green number is your target, and on the last day of the month you should be changing your blue figure for a green one that matches the number of available sessions, in other words hitting your target.

12. On the same whiteboard underneath the 60 minute slots, place a number in green for how many appointments you want to target yourself to generate in that month. Again in blue next to the green figure update the total as you successfully add to your tally. Your mission again is to match the two figures by the end of the month.

13. Now add another figure in green that represents the revenue value you are targeting yourself to generate from that month's meetings that you've attended. Next to it in blue add and update the revenue figure you've achieved as the month progresses.

14. At the end of each month review your performance. Be brutally honest with yourself. Here are some questions you will need to ask.

Did I allow other things to take priority over my call slots?

When on a calling session did I allow distractions to interfere with my calls?

Did I work in a focused way, working systematically through my call list?

Can I honestly say I gave this my very best shot this month?

What went really well on my calls?

What can I improve on?

What did I learn?

Did I set only appointments that were based on a good two way conversation, or did I "force it" at any time?

15. Take action to improve the next month's calls based on your own answers to the above. Self appraisal is your key to your success.

The above 15 step process is all about being accountable. Your figures will not lie. If you've completed the sessions your white board will tell you so, and equally so will your sales figures. Do not allow yourself to make excuses as to why you didn't make your calls. Take responsibility one day at a time and you'll build a really healthy sales pipeline.

The Japanese have a word "Kaizen" for the law of incremental improvement. It means that if each day you make small incremental improvements in your performance the overall effect will be hugely positive. So focus on that day, that session, those calls. Complete the activity, one day at a time and the rest will take care of itself.

After a few months of monitoring your progress like this, you'll be able to pretty accurately predict what your sales pipeline will produce for you. You will be amazed at just how accurate your numbers are. In other you'll know the number of calls it takes to have a conversation with a decision maker, how many conversations will lead to an appointment, and ultimately how many of those appointments will result in sales. It almost becomes like a factory. The raw materials are your discipline, determination, work ethic and of course the calls themselves. The end products are dates in your diary to see potential new customers, an overflowing sales pipeline, and increasing sales revenue. That may sound simplistic but it's just the way it is. Put the work in and telemarketing will always pay you back many times over. However, like all factories if the raw materials stop being delivered then there can be no end product.

Accountability and a few tough words

Taking responsibility is one way to guarantee your success, but another even more powerful characteristic to have is to be accountable for your actions.

Take responsibility for and be accountable for the fact that everything that happens, or does not happen with regard to implementing **Straightforward Approach™** is down to you.

Do not kid yourself, lie to yourself, or cheat or yourself, do not BS yourself or others.

Do the work, make the calls, practice your craft, and enjoy the rewards but don't let yourself off the hook by making excuses if you don't get your head down and make it happen.

Have I have always been 100% responsible and accountable during my sales career? No, of course not, everyone has their off days, and whenever I had them I can tell you that I paid the price. Equally, when I got my head down again, went to basics and realised that if I wanted success the truth was that no one was going to do it for me, my figures just started to sky rocket again. This will be your truth too. Do the work, enjoy the rewards.

Getting a mentor and business coach can be fantastic ways to keep you accountable for your actions particularly if you are running your own business as effectively you are accountable to no one and it's easy to delude yourself.

A good mentor will ask you the tough questions, and not let you off the hook until you have answered them honestly. You're really looking for someone who has already achieved the levels of success that you aspire to-someone who has already "been there and done that". They will be someone who can act as a role model for success and are living proof that it can be done.

I've been fortunate to have met some super successful people over the years and one thing they all exude is **CONFIDENCE** Not particularly in any kind of flash or brash way, but you sense from them that they are certain on where they are going and that success is par for the course, there is an inevitability about it. Get around these people, their attitude will rub off on you.

Many say that you are the average of the five people you spend the most time with. If the five people you are spending the most time with are not positive and supporting your goals and ambitions then if you are to push to the heights that you want to in business, sales and in life you may have to take a serious look at that.

A good business coach will help you to put in place the systems and processes you need in order to make your business a success. These people need not necessarily themselves have achieved super success but they will have a demonstrable track record of helping people to put efficient plans of action in place. After all, many a successful sports coach of elite teams has often never played at the same level themselves but they have a knack of getting others to perform.

OK, sometimes you won't hit the targets you set, as long as you can honestly say you gave it everything then you have nothing to be hard on yourself about.

If however, you know that you've short changed yourself then sort it out, and quickly get back on track.

Final thoughts

At the start of this book I made you a promise that I could provide you with a system that was guaranteed to help you to win more new customers.

With **Straightforward Approach**™ you now have all the tools you need to get on the phone and make it happen.

I don't know you personally so I'm unable to predict to what degree you will throw your effort, commitment, and determination into your outbound calls.

However what I can predict without question is that for those of you that step up to the challenge, have belief in yourself, take on board the concepts tools and tips discussed in this book, and above all take daily consistent action, you will achieve the positive results that you deserve.

I wish you massive success in the future, and remember success is not gained by having knowledge alone, but by having the knowledge and then doing something with it.

Now get on the phone and have some fun!

Contact Robbie Stepney

Robbie Stepney
Maximise Your Phone Confidence™
The Colchester Centre
Hawkins Road
Colchester
Essex
CO2 8JX
Tel: 01206 832 280
E Mail: Enquiries@RobbieStepney.com

www.RobbieStepney.com.

Visit the site to be added to Robbie's VIP e mail list to start receiving periodic powerful information, tips, articles and resources all designed to help you **Maximise Your Phone Confidence™**.

Get in touch and take your sales to the next level.

You can also make enquiries on the number above about booking Robbie to deliver sales training for your Company, or to speak at your event.

Calls That Count Limited
The Colchester Centre
Hawkins Road
Colchester
Essex
CO2 8JX
Tel: 01206 832 280
E Mail: Enquiries@CallsThatCount.co.uk
www.CallsThatCount.co.uk

Robbie is MD of award winning B2B telemarketing Company Calls That Count Limited.

To find out more about how the Calls That Count Team can help to fill your sales pipeline with new sales appointments and leads, or for help and advice on any aspect of B2B telemarketing, call the number above or visit the website to complete a contact request outlining briefly your requirements. A member of the team will then be in touch shortly.

We all have dreams about what we want to achieve in business and in life.

There will always be situations to test us, circumstances that push us to our limits, and reasons why putting our dreams on hold seems like a good idea.

It's at these times that we need to have a single minded resilience, persistence, and a strong belief in ourselves that will enable us to push through each and every barrier put in our way.

One of my dreams was to write a book that people would read one day. Thank you for helping me to achieve it.

What's your dream right now?

Focus on what you want, go for it with everything you have, and don't let anyone tell you that you can't do it.

Robbie Stepney FInstSMM
Colchester, Essex, England
June 2015

Made in the USA
Charleston, SC
05 October 2015